The Lives of the Silent

Stories of Quiet Courage and Connection

The Lives of the Silent

Stories of Quiet Courage and Connection

Andrew Houvouras

KeyPress Publishing

KeyPress Publishing
www.keypresspublishing.com

KeyPress Publishing

This book is a work of nonfiction. Unless otherwise noted, the author and the publisher make no explicit guarantees as to the accuracy of the information contained in this book and in some cases, names of people and places have been altered to protect their privacy.

Copyright © 2025 by Andrew Houvouras
All rights reserved. No part of this publication may be reproduced, stored in a retrieval system, or transmitted in any form or by any means, electronic, mechanical, photocopying, recording, or otherwise without the prior permission of the publisher or in accordance with the provisions of the Copyright, Designs and Patents Act 1988 or under the terms of any license permitting limited copying issued by the Copyright Licensing Agency.

Author: Andrew Houvouras

The Lives of the Silent: Stories of Quiet Courage and Connection

Published by: KeyPress Publishing
Science Adviser: Thomas Freeman
Brand Integrity: Jana Burtner
Production Manager: Adele Hall
Editors: Mary Sproles Martin, Ashley Johnson, Kelly Lee, and Stefanie Carr
Cover Design: Kim Harding
Designer: Jess LaGreca, Mayfly book design

ISBN: 979-8-9886548-9-6 (Paperback); 979-8-9922514-4-9 (Hardcover)

Library of Congress Control Number: 2025934250

Published in Melbourne, Florida
Distributed by:
ABA Technologies, Inc.
930 South Harbor City Blvd, Suite 402
Melbourne, FL 32901
www.abatechnologies.com

KeyPress Publishing books are available at a special discount for bulk purchases by corporations, institutions, and other organizations. For more information, please email keypress@abatechnologies.com.

Table of Contents

A Note on Topics and Names vii

Foreword ix

Preface xv

Acknowledgments xix

Introduction 1

Section 1: Learning the Language of the Silent 9

Chapter 1: Artie 13

Chapter 2: Sabrina 21

Chapter 3: Harry 29

Chapter 4: Robert 39

Section 2: The Silent in a Dangerous World 45

Chapter 5: Jed 49

Chapter 6: Dan 55

Section 3: The Richness of Life Well Lived 63

Chapter 7: JD 67

Chapter 8: Silas 75

Chapter 9: Heidi 85

Chapter 10: Joey 91

Section 4: Navigating Transitions **99**

Chapter 11: Eddie 103

Chapter 12: David 111

Chapter 13: Jason 121

Chapter 14: Jackson 129

Chapter 15: Mr. A. Number 1 141

Conclusion 151

References 155

About the Author 157

A Note on Topics and Names

This book contains stories with swearing and sensitive topics that may be triggering to some readers. A behavior analyst describes in detail what is observed, so I have chosen not to sugarcoat the language that was sometimes used, nor do I gloss over difficult subjects. The silent were always authentic. I want their stories to be authentic as well.

Their names, of course, are not authentic. Names and other details have been changed to protect their privacy.

Foreword

When Andrew first asked me to consider writing a foreword for a book he had begun to write to tell of the lives of some of his past clients, I agreed without hesitation. I first met Andrew when he was a brilliant, highly respected, and indeed beloved behavior analyst in one of our local school systems. Knowing Andrew as I have for perhaps 20 years now, I knew it would be an honest, sincere, deeply personal, and enlightening book that would treat the stories of these individuals with care and sensitivity. What I did not expect was the flood of memories and emotions his book would evoke in me as I read each story.

No human being is exactly like another, of course. As behavior analysts, we come to understand that every person's learning history is so highly individualized that diagnostic categories are at best insufficient and can actually distract us in our effort to discover what has real meaning and value for the individual human being beneath the "behavioral profile." And yet in the stories of the 15 people you are about to meet, I discovered a kind of harmonic resonance with the lives of some of my own past clients, very different but somehow similar people whom I've been lucky enough to encounter during my long career; and through that resonance, these stories somehow triggered memories that I had not touched for many years. In doing this work, my varied relationships with clients have filled me with a sense of duty, joy and laughter, understanding, confusion, compassion, frustration, deep concern, and sometimes even anger at the unfairness of life—and ultimately, they provided me with an abiding amazement at the human capacity to survive challenges most of us can barely imagine.

Yet, at times this work has also filled me with a deep sense of dread—where the responsibility of trying to reach those who have lived a life of such suffering or deep neglect has had me question my own capacity to do justice to the need before me. For in order to survive, many people we meet in our work have learned to withdraw into the safety of their solitude by striking out at others or attempting to harm themselves, behaviors shaped and strengthened by a world where love and affection have been in devastatingly short supply. Coming face-to-face with this reality, I knew that failure was not an option—even knowing that success can sometimes be measured in inches rather than miles. But in the evidence-based world, applied behavior analysis has proven to offer the best approach, this science of human behavior, to help us learn to act in ways that help us live richer and fuller lives, and indeed to unlearn those behaviors that work against our own best interests. No human endeavor is perfect, and positive outcomes can sometimes be elusive. Yet if we persist, we can almost always make things better.

At first, I balked at Andrew's use of the term "the silent." Having worked in a large state institution for the first 15 years of my career, I had always looked at my residential clients as being more invisible than silent—people placed out of sight, where the public could remain unaware of their existence, unaffected, insulated.

For most of the history of these institutions until behavior analysis came along, family members or guardians were gently but firmly advised by the medical professionals that in handing over their troublesome child or young adult into the care of the state, the kindest approach was to let them go, fully and with finality, since maintaining regular contact would make their transition to this new life more difficult. Even when contact was maintained, it was most likely rare and faded out over time. Thus, so many of the people in these situations lived their lives through an ever-changing parade of caregivers, some of whom were kind, but too soon gone; and some of whom were decidedly not kind, and perhaps around for far too long. As for training in a therapeutic approach to the work, well, that is only as effective as the supervision and follow-up that maintain the quality of care. And these residential facilities have a long history of being profoundly under-resourced, with the people within often described as "warehoused." Remember: Invisible.

But as I read through these stories, I came to understand what Andrew was talking about in using the term "the silent." Yes, some of these stories are about people who do not speak. But that is silence on a surface level. We are talking about a deeper silence here, a silence with which we are all familiar, whether we realize it or not. For we have all lived as one of the silent at some time in our lives. Perhaps you grew up as a misunderstood or neglected kid, or a teenager with problems your parents just couldn't get, or you have been in a marriage where trust has been lost and love is just a memory—no matter what, at some point you may have come to feel like an outsider in your own family, your deepest thoughts and yearnings long unspoken. Perhaps you have been bullied in school, the unpopular kid who nobody seems to like—or just maybe you were the most popular kid in class but had to carefully maintain a well-constructed but so very exhausting pretense to hide the secret of a far darker home life than any of your admirers could imagine. Perhaps you have worked in a job where you had to cope with an endlessly dismissive boss, harassing or prejudiced or misogynistic, who always belittled you as being much less than you knew yourself to be. But you were voiceless. Silent.

Some of the people in this book had lived whole lives of this kind of unremitting deeper silence—until people like Andrew came along and unlocked the door. In the lives described in this book, we can perhaps see a reflection of our own unique experience of this personal silence; and looking back, we might just see that at some point, someone appeared in our own life who helped us escape our own silence to speak out at last. Someone unexpected. A friend perhaps, or mentor ... or someone locked away from society whose own suffering in silence somehow revealed and opened the lock on our own deeper voice. Miraculous.

The miracle of this work is not only that we come to find that we are all the same, but in these relationships, we help each other escape the silence. The stories Andrew tells are the stories of human endurance, and compassion, with both successes and failures. But as Andrew tells us again and again without having to say a word about it, in these stories, the teacher is also the student. Everyone is learning, and every lesson carries with it a deeper truth.

And so, as I reflect on what Andrew has written here, I would add a 16th story to the table of contents: the story of Andrew. Throughout these pages, we hear him speak with simple eloquence of the opening of his heart through the time he was blessed to spend with these 15 very different and often challenging people, and doubtless many more not described here; and we find that the therapist receives therapy in the giving, and the gift he receives in return is a gift to his heart and the end of the silence he never knew was there until the people in these stories revealed its presence. In our silence lies a personal truth that strains to be revealed. I know this because Andrew's story resonates with my own. We have walked a similar path to understanding, helped along the way by those who have pointed us toward the road that has not only led to an understanding of who we really are, but who we hope to become.

So here I can now add myself to this book as the 17th story. And as you read these pages, perhaps you will find that you can add your own name to this growing list of the once silent who can now step into the light and live the truths that have been hidden within your own hearts. Contained within these pages are not just the lives of 15 of the silent, kept hidden in the shadows of society and held within the loneliness of their own isolation until they could finally emerge through the love and care of others. These are the stories of us all.

—**Thomas R. Freeman**, MS, BCBA
ABA Technologies, Inc.

Preface

Robert and Harry. That was my first title for a book, an idea that came to me in 1997 when I thought of writing a fictitious story about two friends who grew up in a state institution, based on the lives of two real men. While I was in graduate school, I met Robert and Harry, housemates who had spent years living together in a psychiatric facility prior to moving to a group home together. They were vastly different in appearance and demeanor. Robert was thick, fair skinned, with light blue eyes, a widow's peak, and graying hair. He was quiet, having, to anyone's knowledge, never spoken. Harry was tiny with olive skin, a full head of brown hair, and brown eyes. He spoke often. I liked the idea of the yin of Robert's quietness to the yang of Harry's boisterousness. No matter how much I liked the idea, my attempts to create a story were futile. My ability to write fiction waned with my decreased interest in reading fiction (except for Stephen King). *Robert and Harry* never came to be.

My life grew in its complexity, and I continued to find great interest in my field of work, applied behavior analysis (ABA). I spent much of the following 25 years reading exclusively nonfiction: research articles; textbooks; biographies; and, most importantly, the work of B. F. Skinner. I didn't know at the time that the idea of writing would come back to me when I learned of the passing of the two clients I had loosely cast as Robert and Harry. Looking back on our times together, I was inspired to talk about them and their lives with the realization that truth is always more fascinating than fiction.

• • •

My own journey to help the silent began in an unusual way. In 1986, my father was a Catholic school principal. A family came to him wanting their son, Ronnie, who had autism, to have a Catholic education. At the time, autism was not well-known, and people were inclined to think you said "artistic" and ask you what the person painted, as opposed to understanding the term as describing a developmental disability. The parents had approached several schools in the area about the possibility of Ronnie attending a Catholic school. They had arranged to pay for their own, trained special education teacher to attend school with their son to provide him with academic and behavioral support. Numerous principals told the family the painful truth—they did not understand autism or have the resources to provide Ronnie with an appropriate educational experience—all except one, my father. He could not promise how it would go nor predict the outcome, but he said he and the school would try.

The parents were looking for teenage boys to hire as what they called "peer companions." My brothers and I fit the bill. The job involved basic academic tutoring and providing some assistance and coaching for Ronnie in community activities, sports lessons, and practices after school and on weekends. My identical twin, Matt, was the first of my brothers to begin working with Ronnie.

He quickly took to it. Once soccer and basketball seasons ended, my older brother, Alex, and I became part of the rotation. It would be fortuitous that my youngest brother, Chad, was in the same grade as Ronnie, and the two were classmates who became friends (Chad went on to earn a master's in special education).

Ronnie could speak. His loving family and the many fine professionals they assembled as a team helped him develop his communication skills. "May. I. Have. Pizza. Please," he might say, chaining several words in simple sentences. While Ronnie could speak, he was not conversational. Minutes to hours could go by with him saying very few words. Talking was not easy for him. But time with him was. In my time with him, I received a lifetime of lessons, ones I have carried with me for almost 40 years.

Whatever he lacked in conversational skills, Ronnie made up for in sense of humor. When I would come to his house, he would look at me once and say, "Hello. Andrew." Then he would giggle and start walking fast toward his room and say, "Matthew!" (the name of my identical twin brother). I would run after him and tickle him, declaring, "Say my name right!" Ronnie would say "Matthew, Matthew, Matthew!" until his breath gave way and he would say "Andrew" to get me to stop. Numerous times, I would walk away and hear him whisper "Matthew," and the fun began again.

Ronnie quickly taught me about the most important skill I would need, a skill that I would rely on for decades: the power of observation. When minutes, hours, and days are spent with little spoken language, we become more astute observers of the person and their environment. We abandon the clutter, the clatter, and the need to hear an answer and begin looking for one in the sequences and contingencies that play out before us. I can never thank Ronnie and his family enough for this gift. It first set me on a course to know I wanted to continue working with people like

Ronnie, and I began trying to find a name for this way of thinking. I eventually found my path in the science of human behavior, ABA. Ronnie was my introduction to the silent, which led me to ABA. He and his family gave me an interest and a purpose that has largely defined my own life. I owe so much to my family and to Ronnie's family for the life that chose me.

• • •

The following stories are brief snippets of time representing my memories, which are often flawed, failing things. They are as accurate as I can recall, inevitably shaped, modified, and distorted by the contingencies that produce thoughts and writing and the passage of time. When I submitted the idea for the book, a colleague suggested the title *The Voice of the Silent*. I understood the sentiment but bristled at the suggestion, as I thought people would garble the idea I wanted to convey—that one's voice could be found in one's actions—and, instead, believe I claimed to be the spokesperson for the people portrayed in these pages. I did not. I do not. I was never their voice. What I hope to have been was a patient and kind human being, an astute observer and recorder of our times together.

The stories are shared frozen moments that molded my perspective and inspired a commitment to finding truth, beauty, and inspiration in what I could see. There is great beauty there, if you look for it.

Acknowledgments

Writing a book has allowed me the pleasure of looking back on decades of relationships, friendships built on mutual respect, and a desire to help improve the human condition. As I thank people, there are inevitably people not listed but who matter to me and helped me. If you find yourself as one of those people, please know any omission is unintentional, and I will ask for your grace when we see each other again.

To the Searcy family, I have known for years that I would never meet a family who matched your love and commitment to the greater good. Thank you for introducing me to autism and starting me on this wonderful journey.

To Sherri, Molly, Patrick (RIP), and my Aunt Rebecca, thank you for giving me a love of the written word. How I write is so influenced by your tutelage and grace. The greatest thanks I can give to you is the book itself. You were the epitome of good teachers, and I cannot believe I had the good fortune of having all of you foster my love of language.

To Marc, Jimmie, Curnutte, Margie, Sherry, the late Dr. Ruth Sullivan, and many others, my eternal gratitude for dealing with a young, cocky kid and helping him learn what was really important.

I left for graduate school ready to conquer the world and then learned from all of you that sometimes changing that world in the six-block radius where you live, attend school, and work is enough.

In and around 1998, I met a kindred spirit, Dr. Jose Martinez-Diaz, a behavior analyst who was a fantastic storyteller. He kindled my passion for applied behavior analysis (ABA), but more so my passion for people. Over the next several years, we would trade stories, and he would continue building a program for ABA at Florida Institute of Technology and through his company, ABA Technologies, where he invited me to be a part-time instructor in the ABA Online program, something I have been doing since 2007. Our shared beliefs in one another and the power of behavioral science to produce meaningful change culminated in my becoming the Director of Experiential Training in 2019 and pursuing a PhD.

Jose was responsible, too, for many of my friendships: Tom, Corey, Bill, Kristin, Evette, Jan, Gloria, Bryon, and Stacey. These people are the salt of the earth, people who have dedicated their lives to disseminating ABA to the world. It is no surprise to me that Florida Institute of Technology is the premiere program in providing education in ABA to people globally. While I do not have the data, I am sure they bear out that the team at ABA Technologies and Florida Institute of Technology are responsible for the most certified behavior analysts and assistant behavior analysts in the world.

Following my work in specialized treatment centers, I spent many years working in the public school system. I have worked alongside people who may not be well-known in the field but whose work I have marveled at for decades. I count these people as mentors, professional exemplars, and friends, and their commitment to helping others is exceeded only by their compassion.

To Rene, Kevin, Jayson, Alex, Jennifer C., Oscar, Trish, Lynn, Robin, Tiffany, Leslie, Michelle, Jennifer T., Susan, Celena, Dawna,

Lisa, Angela, and Bill. Thank you for so many good years together. I would like to single out Rene, the single most talented person at working with children I have ever worked with. I could trust her with any case, any task, any truth. Thank you for always being such a great colleague and friend.

To my Florida Association for Behavior Analysis (FABA) family: Merrill, Amy, Nikki, Missy, Yulema, Tiki, Matt, Willie, Karly, Jon, Kevin, and Baker. Over the years, I have become friends with my heroes, all because two of my mentors, Amy-Erin and Donna, insisted I join this tiny (no longer tiny) organization. While we see each other only once or twice a year, please know how much I value our friendships and how your work motivates me to be better.

Many thanks to Rayna, one of the few people whose actual name is used in the book. Thank you for two sons and great memories. Watching you work with the silent was an absolute treat. I enjoyed learning from you almost as much as I enjoyed watching you parent our sons.

To my colleagues at Florida Institute of Technology: Kim, Eb, Mark, Dave, Kaitlynn, Jonathan, Katie, Nic, Fredenburg, and Linda. Thank you for taking a chance on me and allowing me to be part of the team. I am in awe of all of you. Particular thanks to Eb, who was a mentor to me and dared me to experiment. And thank you to Mark for your friendship and encouragement. You were the first person to help me get published, and you continue to be a cherished friend.

To "Doc" Lilianne. So many of our conversations helped steer this book toward completion. Thank you for being a beacon of light and providing me with a fresh perspective when I really needed it.

To my mother, Jane—the best person I know. Years into her teaching career, I remember her, as an art teacher with classes of over 25 students, sending the one-on-one assistant for a student with autism spectrum disorder on a break during art class. When asked why, she replied, "I have to figure out how to teach him." I still cannot fathom how lucky I am to be your son.

To my father, Drew. Had you not taken a tremendous leap of faith, challenging yourself, your teachers, and your students to learn about a person with autism, I may not have gone down this path, and this book may have never been written. We share so much: a name, a love of the ocean, sea glass collections (my father has the greatest sea glass collection I have even seen). Thank you for always being there.

Of the many gifts my parents gave me, none were greater than my four best friends, my brothers, Alex, Matt, Brian, and Chad. Of the five of us, I am by far the least talented, least creative, and least accomplished. Their accomplishments in their fields and their passions could fill pages. I am lucky they chose different career paths, or I would be the fifth-best behavior analyst in my own family. I am so incredibly proud of each of you.

To my sons, Preston and Kooper. Thank you for giving my life greater purpose. Preston, the old soul trapped in the body of a younger guy: Your wisdom and ability to navigate through life befriending and being kind to people has always made me proud. Your kindness is matched only by your intellect and work ethic. Thank you for being a wonderful son. Kooper, you have always been your own man, leading and not following. It has not always made your life easy, but your tenacity, strength of conviction, heart, and belief in self are awesome to behold. I don't know what I ever did to deserve a son like you.

Lastly, this book would never have been written without my dearest of friends, Christi, a brilliant behavior analyst, a staunch advocate for those in need of one, a dedicated teacher of the science of behavior, and the kindest of souls. The detours in our personal lives led to many phone calls, coaching one another through our new normal. And they led to me gaining the "bestest" girl Frenchie in the world, Poppy. Much of this book is the result of us "talking story" in search of peace during tumultuous times. I can never thank you enough.

Introduction

In a world full of noise, there live the silent.

This book is about people very much like you and me. They laugh, aspire, cry, and have preferences. They love, hurt, feel, and experience the world. But their journeys through this life are more challenging than most because of what they do not or cannot say. "Shy," "nonverbal," "nonvocal," and "speech impaired"—the terms used to describe these people are all attempts to convey the idea of a pervasive quietness that marked much of their time and many of their interactions with me.

The term "the silent" used here is a deliberate choice. We tend to speak about people by providing a label to them: "He's the bald, White man," or "He's the tall, Black man," or "She's autistic."

Over the decades, people have described others who do not speak or have trouble learning from traditional educational environments as "psychotic," "disturbed," "insane," "deaf and dumb," "retarded," and "profoundly impaired." Once a label is affixed to a particular person, we may forego names and niceties and simply refer to that person by that label. A label reduces the complexity of a person to a single word or phrase.

While terms are necessary to explain and understand phenomena—and to provide a common language for discussion—the lack of consideration to choose terms with sensitivity and humanity reflects an indifference to the plight of those in need. The silent need additional support and specialized assessments and intervention, but historically, the extent of the "support" was primarily the silent being given pejorative labels.

The purpose of a diagnosis is to identify a condition. The labels given to the silent seem to define what the person *has*, even though diagnoses are largely based on what someone *does* or *cannot do*. This was a contradiction I could not escape: We were making inferences about mental processes and difficulties with conclusions based on our observations of the person's behavior—their actions. If this is the case, then adopting an empirical, behavioral orientation seems to be the more prudent approach.

One of the things that appealed to me about the behavior-analytic approach was it never proposed to cure anyone. (Besides, if we're talking about autism, what are we curing anyway?) Behavior analysis emphasizes individualized assessments and behavior plans. The behavior-analytic approach is focused on helping people expand their communicative repertoires, enhance their adaptive behaviors, and develop self-help skills. It aids individuals in developing their self-chosen goals and then helps them develop strategies and skills to move them toward their self-selected, chosen outcomes. What's not to like about that?

My oldest son was born with hemophilia, yet to refer to him as a "hemophiliac" ignores the nuances of his life that combine to make him who he is. He is also a student, an athlete, a son, a grandson, a brother, a cousin, a friend, a coworker, and a thinker. We are all so much more than whatever label someone else gives us.

In thinking back on my experiences working with the silent, minutes to hours could go by with little said. Yes, I, like other staff, parents, and teachers, would speak to my clients, but there were extended voids without words or any noise. Many friends and colleagues have observed that the one thing they craved at the end of many workdays was conversation, as it was often noticeably absent when working with the silent.

There are many ways in which people are silenced. Being born with disabilities is one cause—some unique biological and genetic makeups sometimes interact with the environment in a manner that is inefficient and stymies the development of verbal behavior. One of the diagnostic criteria for autism spectrum disorder, for example, is "communication impairment." "The silent" describes the reality that those with minimal communication are consigned to a life where they may talk minimally or not at all. Consequently, when a person does not speak, others are less likely to talk to them. When you are not speaking, signing, or exchanging pictures, it is difficult to participate in the usual reciprocating give-and-take of communication, and others in the environment are less apt to speak, sign, or exchange pictures with you. What was already a difficult proposition becomes reinforced by the failure of the environment.

The difficulty of having a disability impair communication is not the only way in which people are silenced. People who were sexually and physically abused are often silenced. They may not have lost their voice, but their consent is silenced—the violations and intrusions on their persons, the failure to honor their "No," and their loss of control over their own bodies may serve to confuse and punish further attempts at communicating. If the person's attempts at communicating fail or are punished, what recourse do they have other than to remain silent, or perhaps engage in some other, possibly disruptive behavior, that effectively ends the interaction and keeps others at a safe distance? Having never endured these horrors, I shudder to think about it. I try to analyze how the past affects a person, with silence being a possible consequence.

Silence can also be institutionalized. Psychiatric wards, state institutions, and prison systems often serve to keep those on the fringes of society separate from the rest, isolated, and silent. A person may be ostracized, never invited, unable to join, or turned away by virtue of their diagnosis and behaviors. Even after the Civil Rights Act of 1964 was passed, advocates for individuals with autism had to fight to gain access to public education for them (U.S. Office of Special Education Programs, 2007). The silent were removed from society, and unlike a person serving a prison sentence, the truly silent could be confined for life, innocent of any crime other than being different. This removal often lasted well beyond the sentence of a person who committed a criminal offense who was then free to pursue their life.

The term "the silent" encompasses the interactions and the minutes, hours, and days spent in pursuit of understanding others—interactions that were not necessarily marked by vocal communication. "The silent" implies people sharing moments and working to understand one another without necessarily talking. Was that difficult at times? Yes. Was it impossible? No. Examining what people do, as opposed to what they say, can sometimes provide more relevant information than mere words spoken aloud.

The term also provides clarity: When we strip away the banter, focus on the person and the person's actions, and discard the labels, we open up to the possibilities of what can be discovered through observation, which can then lead to measurement, which can then lead to analysis.

INTRODUCTION

• • •

The stories I tell here are true, taken from the earlier part of my career in the 1990s, when I lived and worked in the southern part of the United States. During graduate school, I primarily worked for an agency providing residential services to individuals on the autism spectrum as a direct-care professional and assistant group home manager. The agency was instrumental in finding people homes. Several of those we helped had been longtime residents of state institutions.

De-institutionalization was a movement that gained steam in the 1970s when investigative journalists exposed some of the horrors taking place within institutions, including insect infestation, the absence of proper medical care, beatings, and sexual assault (Anthony & Leff, 1979). This raised public awareness, and policies shifted toward demanding a better quality of life for those affected. While it took years, large institutions eventually shuttered as the residents began moving into what were commonly referred to as *group homes*—houses where residents with similar characteristics (age, disabilities, and needs) lived, often with varying degrees of professional assistance from adults living or working in the homes. Group homes typically have three to eight residents and an around-the-clock presence of staff, with the ratio of staff to residents varying based on the needs of the residents at that time of day. The homes are often named based on their appearance or location.

In these stories, I describe my work at three group homes, and I have intentionally obscured some details to protect privacy. When I attended graduate school, I first worked in the capacity as a direct-care staff member, then worked as an assistant group home manager at two group homes, and finally returned to work as a direct-care staff member when the demands of graduate school necessitated stepping down as an assistant manager. One of the group homes was in close proximity to the university I was attending, while the other two were close to a large, tree-lined park that occupied a beautiful part of the same city.

My time in graduate school was formative. It was there that I was introduced to the principles of applied behavior analysis (ABA), and my daily work provided rich examples of the concepts I was poring over in textbooks and research journals. The silent imparted daily lessons and provided examples of why a behavioral perspective best addressed their needs: because it did not involve self-reporting and therapist-client dialogue; rather, it relied on objective observation, data collection, and visual inspection of existing trends in graphed data. The more I worked with the silent and the more I learned about ABA, the more sure I was that this was what I wanted to pursue.

After graduate school, I moved back to Florida. My first job as a behavior therapist was at "the center"—a residential treatment facility where children with various disabilities lived year-round. There were five behavior analysts on the staff. Two were colleagues and three were mentors. My three and a half years there were instrumental in cementing my behavioral and ethical leanings. Every day there was a new challenge, as the children were admitted most often due to severe self-injurious and aggressive behaviors; sleeping problems; and the need for intensive, one-to-one support.

It was here that I learned the most about the importance of professional collaboration. The center had diverse treatment teams composed of a psychiatrist, a nurse, a behavior analyst, a speech-language pathologist, and a special education teacher. (If I play well with others, it is because of the training and mentorship I received here.)

Within the center were particular units where children were grouped by age, presenting behavioral concerns, and diagnoses. Each unit had a nurses station to provide 24-hour nursing care, and the bathroom, kitchen, playroom, and closet doors were all locked. When children made sufficient progress, the center had a single group home where children, typically in their teens, could transition. This less restrictive setting was 25 minutes from the campus.

My years here were my immersion into ABA. The classes I took, the assessments I completed, the interventions I implemented, the books and journals I read, and the daily progress of the clients reinforced my growing passion for behavioral science and its profession.

The stories contained within this book represent those silenced by either being unable to actually speak, or by being isolated from society through placement in an institution, removal from a familiar school, or being sent to a specialized center far from home. The stories I tell are theirs. I hope I have honored them by sharing how meaningful their lives were to me and, even if it was never said directly to them, that I will always hold them close to my heart.

SECTION 1
Learning the Language of the Silent

While in my master's program in clinical psychology, I was primarily occupied with school, studying, and work, spending time as a direct-care professional and assistant group home manager. As I progressed through the program, I had several courses on assessment and diagnosis. I was interested in working with individuals with autism, developmental disabilities, intellectual impairments, and severe problem behavior, but the more I learned, the more concerned I became. Standardized and projective (i.e., requiring inference and speculation through vocal responses) tests and instruments were the common tools for assessing people. Unfortunately, for people with smaller vocabularies or with minimal or no spoken language, these instruments revealed little.

While studying psychology, I wrestled with why so many assessments and therapies openly stated their incapacity to accurately evaluate the abilities of the silent. During my time in college and especially graduate school, books explicitly stated the limits of psychologically oriented perspectives in treating the people I found to be the most interesting, the most difficult, and the most in need of support. Many of the people I was assisting did not respond to traditional evaluations and therapies. Traditional psychology readily conceded what it could not do for the silent. Although I loved psychology (and still do), at this time, it failed the people I wanted to assist and so it failed me.

For a few decades, I have said "individuals with autism," and I will continue to use this throughout the book. If a person prefers to be referred to as "autistic," I honor and respect that. None of the people written about in the book ever stated a preference for being called something other than their name. I have made a deliberate decision to write more about what people did versus what labels were given to them.

As mentioned earlier, this book contains stories with swearing and sensitive topics that may be triggering to some readers. A behavior analyst describes in detail what is observed, so I have chosen not to sugarcoat the language that was sometimes used, nor do I gloss over difficult subjects. The silent were always authentic. I want their stories to be authentic as well.

With the silent, we must rely on direct observation. We follow the person with our eyes and listen with our ears, unconcerned about what they scored on a piece of paper. The evidence we need is right before us. Anyone watching can see and hear the same thing. The process is inductive: We observe and allow data to drive our decisions. This signals to the silent a testimony that we respect them and care enough that we are willing to pay extremely close attention to what they do, how they move, where they are on their life journey, and what they say to help make determinations about what goals to set, assessments to select, and treatments to use.

At the same time that I was struggling with the dearth of answers from psychology, behavior analysts were quietly ushering in revolutionary concepts supported by powerful and careful experimental evaluations. As the number of diagnoses of autism climbed, behavioral science responded, demonstrating different ways to assess client preference. For individuals with varying communication difficulties, behavior analysts developed three different general processes for identifying favorite foods, drinks, and activities.

The assessments for preference were accompanied by *functional analysis*, a process of arranging the environment in specific ways to remove the guesswork and allow analysts to identify the consequences that strengthen problem behavior. The advent of this powerful assessment led to the development of interventions derived directly from the assessment, *function-based interventions*, which consistently demonstrated not only an improvement in the behavior for thousands of individuals but also a reduction in the use of punishment. The field was accelerating at a rapid pace, and it was exciting to see where behavioral science would go. It was an innovative time, and my studies and work experiences intermingled to enhance my behavior-analytic repertoires.

Behavior analysis did not and does not offer every answer. Its insistence on direct observation fit the deterministic position I was learning to adopt, affirming that there was nothing wrong with the person—rather, there was a need to find out the person's motivations, what sequences worked, what variables were contributing to the problem, and how to help organize the environment to foster positive behavior change. The empirical observation approach of behavior analysis was consistent with my idea that we could learn about people who said little or whose words did not always match their actions. The stories of Artie, Sabrina, Harry, and Robert are about people silenced by being largely nonspeaking (Artie, Robert, and Sabrina), or having been isolated from society by being placed in institutions (Artie, Harry, and Robert), or being removed from a school system (Sabrina). All of their stories, I hope, reflect the empathy and wonderment that comes when we choose to observe.

CHAPTER 1

Artie

Life outside the walls of an institution was unfamiliar for several of the silent. It certainly was for Artie, who spent 70 years living in state institutions. Those of us who have never been locked away often speculate about how it must have felt when facilities were shuttered and the silent moved outside of the institutional walls into communities. We claim victories when the silent are allowed to remain in their neighborhood public school or when a group home opens in a neighborhood. But those small wins are not ours—they belong to the silent.

We like to imagine a world where the silent are free from suffering, isolation, and apathy, but that world has never existed and probably never will. The most important opinion—that of the silent—is never spoken. We must surmise meaning, inclination, and intent from their behaviors. By virtue of their actions and accomplishments, the silent are the greatest advocates for the importance of observation and a natural science approach to human behavior. Their lives, their intents, and their purpose are found in their deeds. We should count ourselves lucky to be able to know the silent, people like Artie, and to interact and observe how they relate to the world around them.

• • •

Artie was 81 years old when I met him. A client in the agency's group home, he was less than 5 feet tall, although with the slight hunch in his back, he looked even shorter. He was thin, with a tiny bit of white hair and the normal aging spots and wrinkles of an octogenarian. He walked with a distinct, extremely short shuffle. Artie had no teeth, a tragedy that occurred during the days before patients' rights were considerations. Apparently, he was a biter, and the institution prevented biting not through careful assessment and intervention but through extracting his teeth—all of them. His gums were so tough that he could actually chew meat. The agency considered him retired, and his schedule was not as full as those of the other residents.

Artie defined the silent for me: He clearly could understand what we said, but he made no efforts to speak, babble, or echo. I often wondered if he ever had.

Institutions and state hospitals for the insane (a term given to those at the far ends of the normal distribution) must have been frightening places when Artie first was taken into state care: gated and locked communities filled primarily with adults suffering from any number of developmental, psychological, and psychiatric conditions. There were few to no therapies, diagnoses, medications, or education. The idea of rehabilitation was just that: only an idea. Rights were quietly surrendered at the door. It is hard to fathom how such a young child would fit into such an environment. It must have been torturous to the family and terrifying to the little boy who was Artie, who could not speak, sign, or otherwise indicate his trepidation, angst, and loss. To this day, a lump forms in my throat when I think about what Artie's life was like for decades. He was mislabeled and misunderstood. The silent paid the price for an ignorant society and carried those burdens for far too long by themselves.

In 1988, Artie moved into the group home.

Here is the story about Artie's life that had been passed down as an oral history by his late sister, Eleanor. Artie was born in 1913, and his childhood presented his parents with the arduous task of trying to help their son when no one understood much about his condition. One day, when he was 5 years old, his family found him hanging from the ledge of the second story of the family home. Frightened of the prospect of him doing harm to himself or dying—and with no real information about Artie's particular needs or condition available during this time period—his parents did the only thing people in their situation had available to them: They had him declared insane and placed in a state institution.

Most of us cannot fathom this world into which Artie was born. Psychology and psychiatry were in their infancy, and there was little help for people with disabilities or their families. Many of the disabled were relegated to a life of silence. So much information that we take for granted as common knowledge now was unknown at that time. Disabilities were not well understood and rarely discussed. Autism was not widely adopted as a separate condition until Artie was 30 years old.

So, with no understanding, no diagnoses, no expertise, no advocacy, no organizations, and no research, 5-year-old Artie was declared insane and warehoused with strangers. He was consigned to a silent life, confined to the walls of a place that smothered sound, drowned out hope, and removed the silent away from one indifferent world to another: hidden from polite society.

Those of us who spent time with Artie were unsurprised by the story of how he landed in the institution. In spite of his advanced age and frailty, Artie was regarded as an acrobat. Staff had to remain within arm's length of him, not just because of his age-related absence of balance but due to his penchant for attempting to climb on things. Prior to going to bed every night, he would engage in an unusual ritual of trying to get the covers on just right, which often included him doing repeated stretches, placing his left side down on the bed with his left arm outstretched away from his bed and doing a sweeping motion with the arm. This would often be followed by attempting somersaults in bed.

While Artie was incredibly quiet through most of his daily existence, he would get terribly irritated with staff if we gently redirected him from his somersaults. He would make a loud yell and then swing a haymaker at anyone who dared interrupt his nightly ritual—although from our perspective, the ritual was unpredictable and ever-changing. His punch was less a danger and more a "Leave me alone!" gesture. If staff walked to the closet to get a towel, Artie would try to quickly do his "gymnastics" routine before they could intervene. We had many nights when the staff had to scramble to support Artie, genuinely amused by his mischievous nature.

When Artie passed away, the agency staff wrote a beautiful obituary paying tribute to his life. It suggested Artie was liberated when he moved from the institution to the group home. Living life with a disability is partly defined by an attempt to maintain sameness, and so it is impossible for any of us to know if moving to the group home was truly liberating for Artie. He left the only home he had known for 70 years to come to the agency. I want to believe he was set free, but, as it is with the silent, speculation is all that we have.

CHAPTER 1: ARTIE

Over the years, I have talked to gentlemen who lived in institutions and then moved into community group homes. Many said the institution was where they preferred to live. There were always things to do, no one resented them, and everyone was like them.

Artie's was a simple life. He loved to clean, sweep his bedroom, and take out the trash. He would often attempt *to create* trash. He would gather random items from around the house or tear up the newspaper and throw what he found into the garbage, because once it was full, he would be able to walk it out to the trash can. One of Artie's favorite activities was coloring. He would use crayons, pressing them firmly on the paper, filling the entire sheet with color, and then walk to the garbage can to dispose of the paper. Artie would make himself vomit in the kitchen in order to try to quickly get paper towels to clean it up or scurry to get a mop. Not wanting to reinforce the vomiting behavior, we had a rule that Artie could not clean up self-induced vomit.

Artie loved to shave, but his aging, trembling hand required assistance from staff. Many evenings, we would go to his bathroom, where he would eagerly reach for and apply an overabundance of shaving cream across his face prior to enjoying a shave. When done rinsing his face, he would carefully stare into the mirror and joyously rub his hands over his face to ensure every spot was smooth. Artie also enjoyed walking in the beautiful park in the city's center, where he regularly fed the ducks. He walked the mall when the weather prevented outside strolls. He was well cared for, treated with great respect, and adored by everyone in the agency.

In the summer of 1995, my coworkers and I took Artie and several other residents of the group home to North Carolina's Outer Banks. It was one of the few vacations Artie had been on in his entire life. The agency had rented a house a few blocks from the beach in Kill Devil Hills. The house was elevated on stilts, as many homes are in this hurricane-affected area. Large, covered porches encircled the home on the second floor. I remember distinctly how much time Artie spent on the porch in a rocking chair, just rocking time away. It was soothing, and Artie was relaxed, contented to enjoy the slow time of his retirement.

One of the things about that particular trip that was really meaningful was the fact that, to the best of everyone's knowledge, this was the first time he'd ever set foot on the beach—at 81 years old. I remember being assigned to him on the day we went to the beach and how gingerly he took each step because of the unfamiliar feeling of the sand beneath his feet. Artie seemed unsure of himself and held onto my hand tightly, something he rarely did on our many walks at parks. He really loved the water, and I remember taking him to the ocean to swim and float. On several occasions, we walked to the pier, where he seemed to take great joy in being perched high above the beach, looking down at the unfamiliar sights before him.

I wonder what it must have been like for him at 81 to experience the beach for the very first time in his life. I was lucky to have been there to accompany him. As someone who has spent much of his life at the beach and in the ocean, I was so happy to share this with him, even if it was in his later years. I can only imagine what it meant to Artie. I am so grateful for the time I was able to spend with him and for the lessons he taught me.

Of Artie's many wonderful qualities and idiosyncrasies, the last part of his nighttime ritual was unchanging and happened every single night without fail. After a bath and dressing for bed, Artie would put away any laundry and check the garbage to see if he needed to make a run to the trash cans, and then he would look for his white sneakers. Artie wore white sneakers almost every day, and they were a prized possession. Every night, after he located his shoes, he would bend down slowly and gingerly until he was on his hands and knees. Then he would begin pushing his sneakers all the way back to the corner where the walls met. Once they hit the back wall, he would continue pushing as if to ensure they were as far back, as hidden from view as they could possibly be.

Some might pass this off as some type of behavior paired with autism or a kind of perseverative obsessive-compulsive type of behavior. Those of us who knew Artie, however, thought differently. As he and his housemates fell asleep, we would hypothesize as to "whys." Our anecdotal conclusion, based on no data other than the knowledge of his decades living in an institution, was that Artie learned he would have to hide the things that were valuable to him, or they would be gone. Putting his shoes so far back, well out of view, guaranteed they would be there when he woke up the next day.

While I saw this ritual play out dozens and dozens of times, it always amazed me that while he never spoke a single word and lived a life that most of us cannot and do not want to imagine, Artie was wise enough to value the things he had and took care of his few possessions. It spoke to his resiliency and reminded me daily of the things he had overcome.

Artie and his white shoes had an impact on me: I wear my white shoes whenever I attend conferences. This has been my private homage to my friend, which I am sharing now for the first time.

Artie was affectionate. I don't mean that he was prone to more outward expressions of affection such as hugs, but when around preferred people, he would take his hand (usually the right hand) and reach to caress their cheek. Artie's circle was small, and receiving this form of affection from him was a powerful recognition of being accepted, liked, and welcomed into that tiny group of people to whom he extended his hand in friendship. It was a rite of passage only the lucky experienced.

Artie was sometimes impatient. Sabrina, one of the two women living in the home, was often on the receiving end of his impatience. If she said, "Artie!" anywhere in his presence, he would yell, raise his hand, and attempt to hit her. He then would chase her angrily in the halls as she ran away with a huge smile, knowing she had gotten a reaction from him. Artie could also hold a grudge. After Sabrina had irritated him, if he was sweeping the kitchen floor and she walked by, he would swing the broom at her.

All of the things Artie did were unique to him; he had quite the repertoire of actions produced by his environments and learning history. The uniqueness of Artie and his responses to the world around him remind us that the silent and the speaking are the same. We are all human beings with large, diverse ranges of behaviors, capabilities, challenges, preferences, and idiosyncrasies. The speaking world tends to label, name, categorize, and speak about the silent in the way we discuss Artie: driven to try to understand a life without a spoken word.

If this tendency drives the development of ways to assess, educate, and treat, it is a worthwhile endeavor. If not, it harkens back to the time when Artie, the child, was declared insane and placed in an institution, reduced to being defined only by the label given to him by others. He, like all of us, was always more than a label. Artie's tale reminds us that while he could not speak, his life was quietly spectacular, meaningful, important, and memorable.

CHAPTER 2

Sabrina

There are some people in the world whose behaviors make you anxiously await what they will do next. The element of surprise can be particularly reinforcing. Just as people who speak words that make you giggle or sit with your jaw open, there are those who are silent who continue to fill the world with those "Did that just really happen?" moments.

Few people in my private universe have surprised me as much as Sabrina did. While our relationship was marked by mutual respect, fun, and hard work, she routinely behaved in ways that befuddled me, filling each shift with the prospect of endless possibilities. Behavioral science prides itself in predicting the likelihood of given actions. In my time with Sabrina, the only thing I could accurately predict was that, during the times she was awake, I could expect the unexpected.

• • •

"Stop!" yelled a heavyset White woman, her hand outstretched in the universal "stop" motion. "I have a cousin with Down Syndrome, and you are hurting that girl!"

It must have been quite a sight: a 6-foot-3, 300-pound Black man and a 5-foot-10, 185-pound White man with a shaved head, arms intertwined as we flanked a 4-foot-11 White woman with curly dark hair, fair skin, and loose clothing.

"Ma'am," said my coworker, Gavyn, "Please move out of the way."

I followed up with "Ma'am, we work for the local autism agency, and if you have concerns, call 555-1212."

Our well-meaning citizen was a few minutes late in helping. Inside the small department store, Sabrina had ripped a substantial chunk of hair out of a female staff member's head. While shopping, Sabrina had come across a plastic baby doll. She said, "Baby doll, get," in what were a few of the approximately 20 words in her vocabulary. When the staffer told her "No," she reached her hands up, grabbed the staff member's long brown hair, and dropped to the ground. Gavyn and I were about 20 feet away with our *clients* (the residents whom we cared for), and we quickly hurried over. It took a few minutes to peel the hair out of Sabrina's grip. We were then using our agency-approved escort procedure to exit the store when our collective appearance startled this poor lady.

Sabrina, with her light blue eyes and curly, messy black hair, was well-known in the local autism community in the 1990s due to the sheer intensity of her behavior despite her small physical stature. We met shortly after she aged out of the local school system, and we were both in our mid-20s. The local schools had been unable to educate her. The agency, often willing to step up, worked to get her a place in the group home, assigned her two adult staff members, and insisted they could come up with appropriate programming.

CHAPTER 2: SABRINA

Of the many clients I worked with, Sabrina stood alone in regard to concerning, aggressive behavior. Her outbursts came in many forms: hair pulling, biting, kicking, and scratching. When I first began working with her, she had been aggressive toward a female staff member when asked to shower. We switched clients, and when I insisted Sabrina begin her shower, the aggressive behaviors were directed toward me. My left hand bears one of the few scars I have from this time, from when she dug her nails into my skin. Social media is replete with stories of people wearing scars as badges of honor. I wear mine differently. They remind me of my failures: failure to plan, failure to observe, failure to predict, and failure to hear the silent. Whether with Sabrina or someone else, there were times I failed. The scars are permanent reminders of my humanity and of the grip the environment has on behavior.

On Sunday mornings, Sabrina's mother, Sylvia, often rode the city bus to the group home to visit. She had long hair, dyed jet black, and would arrive at the group home dressed in her Sunday best. She would often bring snacks and treats, and periodically, contraband: plastic dolls and other items we asked her not to bring. Sabrina seemed to prefer brief visits, so she would quickly grab and explore the bag her mother brought her; say "Baby doll, get"; and, after being calmly redirected several times, typically sit on the couch with her doll and rock back and forth. The visits never lasted very long, as neither Sabrina nor her mother had well-developed leisure repertoires.

"I forgot" was the common reply when Sylvia gave Sabrina something she was not supposed to have. Sabrina was fond of small dolls, but she routinely used them in a manner that resulted in self-harm. Those who study behavior often learn grandma was right: Absence *does* make the heart grow fonder. In more scientific terms, this is just another way of saying that being deprived of something increases its value as a *reinforcer*, something following a behavior that increases the chances a person will do things to produce it. There was no choice but to limit Sabrina's access to small plastic dolls, but as a result, she would want them even more.

One Sunday during a visit, Sylvia asked if she could play the piano. All the agency's group homes had pianos in the front rooms. It was part of the effort, in addition to well-kept lawns, to have the homes look appealing and fit in well with their neighborhoods. The staff was thrilled, since Sabrina's visits with her mom were usually quiet affairs. Sylvia sat down on the piano bench. Sabrina sat on the floor to her left, leaning on her elbows and supporting her head with her hands. The sounds of church music filled the air for about a minute or so, when Sylvia abruptly stopped, flung her hands toward her daughter, and said in a thick Southern accent, "Demons, be gone!" Sabrina did not respond, but the staff was in shock.

The group home manager discretely asked Sylvia to speak with him. He asked her, "Sylvia, what are you doing?" to which she replied, "I was peformin' an exorcism." The group home manager, a kind, thoughtful professional, gently said, "Sylvia, we've talked about this. Sabrina isn't possessed. She's autistic. It's how God made her. She just learns differently than you and me." Sylvia was temporarily quiet about the issue but would occasionally still ask the staff, "Why don't she talk? What do you think is wrong with her?" They would mention autism and how Sabrina was special.

Being denied access to things she wanted was problematic for Sabrina, and she often responded with severe episodes of aggressive behavior. Sabrina would approach her staff and say, "Baby doll, get!" When adults would redirect her, she would sometimes plug her fingers in her ear, walk away for just a moment, and return with the same order: "Baby doll, get!" Tears would well in her eyes, her cheeks would flush, and she would cry, "Baby doll, get!" Staff were taught to be calm and to gently let her know what items and activities were available in order to redirect her. On an almost daily basis, these redirections only incensed Sabrina, and she would lash out toward her staff, often scratching, pulling hair, slapping, or attempting to bite. The bites would leave large pressure bruises, the scratches drew blood, and staff with hair (mostly female) had strands of hair pulled out. As we were primarily staffed with college students, early weekend shifts were trying, particularly as staff were often exhausted from staying up late. I recall one of our female staff members coming in after a late night. Sabrina required a shower.

The staff member approached her and said, "Sabrina, it's time for you to take a shower."

"Nooooo," came her reply.

"Sabrina, I just can't this morning." Then she got closer, pointed her finger, and raised her voice. "You need to take a shower!"

"Nooooo!" Sabrina said.

"Sabrina!"

Before the staff member could utter another word, Sabrina reached up, took the aide's brown hair in her hands, and dropped quickly to the ground. With both young women on the ground, other staff moved in quickly to begin the arduous process of trying to remove Sabrina's hands from the hair. During these episodes, Sabrina would often close her eyes, tighten her grip, and attempt to scratch the hands of whoever was attempting to separate her hands from the person's hair.

If not aggressive in her response, Sabrina would sob loudly, tears pouring as she repeated the phrase again and again: "Baby doll, get. Baby doll, get." Knowing what I know now, I wish we had applied behavior analysis (ABA) to guide us in understanding the behavior and had been wise enough to know to teach her some type of alternative behavior. Sabrina would fixate on something, and with only a few words in her vocabulary, it was difficult to determine what she wanted. The intensity of her voice and behavior would escalate as she would repeat again and again what she wanted—although we often didn't understand exactly what she was requesting.

Overnight shifts were covered by two adults, who were required to stay awake to safety monitor the six residents. One cold, snowy winter night around 1:30 a.m., I was sleeping peacefully at my home about 200 yards from the group home and the phone rang. I reached for the phone, hoping this was not another middle-of-the-night call to see if I knew where the mayonnaise was (yes, that actually happened). The staff member on the other end of the line said, "Andrew, we have a problem. Sabrina got up, said 'car,' ran out the back door, and is sitting in the snow. She is refusing to move."

I sprang up, put on winter clothing, and jogged over to the group home. In the back of the group home, sitting in the driveway, was Sabrina, dressed only in her nightgown. Her head was down, and she was lightly thrusting her neck up and down in an involuntary tic. She was unresponsive to what I was saying. The temperature was in the mid-20s. I said to the staff, "We are going to have to try and physically assist her inside if she doesn't go in on her own." One more time, we tried to see if we could prompt Sabrina inside.

"Sabrina, it is very early morning, and we cannot go in the car. It's cold outside, and we need to go in," I said. Sabrina did not respond, orient, or appear to acknowledge what I said. With the slipperiness of the snow and ice, we were worried about physically assisting her. We discussed our positioning, what we would do if she "went dead weight," and how we would then operate off a predetermined three-count action. Just as we got on either side of her, Sabrina stood up, looked down to the snow, took a deep breath, and walked inside. Sleep denied, but crisis averted.

One morning, the group home manager was checking the clients' rooms. When he entered Sabrina's room, he found a small plastic doll. Most of the time, the logical guess would be that Sabrina's mom had brought it "by accident," but Sylvia had not visited in the last 2 weeks, so the manager began questioning the staff. No one admitted to bringing it. He waited for the afternoon shift to arrive, but their answers were the same.

"Guys, I know where these dolls come from," our manager said. "They sell them just down the street. If no one owns up to it by the end of the weekend, I will go review the store's security footage."

When the weekend ended, no one had come forward, so the group home manager, being a man of his word, went to the store while I remained at the group home overseeing the day's activities. Less than an hour after leaving, he returned, looking stunned.

He said, "I just can't believe it. I went to the store and met with the manager. The security cameras show Sabrina walking into the store unaccompanied. She walks in, goes up to where the dolls are, looks at them, picks them up, walks around to the drinks, picks up a drink, and walks out of the store."

As odd as this scenario is, it is not a story about shoplifting. To get to the store, Sabrina had to have exited the group home and walked a few hundred yards down an alley to cross one of the busiest streets in the city. She would then have had to navigate any traffic, go through the parking lot, and walk into the store. She would have repeated those actions in reverse to get home. She somehow did all of this without being seriously hurt or arrested, and without her staff knowing she had left. I can only describe it as a miracle that she did not seriously hurt herself, as Sabrina never showed the ability to cross the street. Quite the opposite, staff had to always be vigilant with her in parking lots and on walks, as she walked quickly with a forward lean, her head down, seemingly oblivious to her surroundings.

As someone who spoke only a few words, she never could tell us the tale, but thankfully, she lived through it.

After looking at the time and date, we identified the staff on duty that day. Sabrina had absconded during the shift change, when the group home had been most chaotic. It was a staff member who was, at best, incompetent. This is the same staff member who was assigned to Artie. On that day, the staff member was reading the paper and when Artie got up, I said, "When he gets up, you need to get up."

The staff member said, "Yessir," and turned his attention back to his newspaper. During our discussion with him about the incident with Sabrina, he said, "I'm sorry. I didn't mean to."

His time with the agency was over.

CHAPTER 3

Harry

The ability of people to adapt to different environments has always astonished me. The pursuit of learning more about what enables people to learn and to modify their repertoires led me to a career in behavioral science. Working with people like Harry was instrumental in continuing to shape my behavior-analytic repertoires. Harry had difficult life circumstances and spent years removed from societal norms, yet he seemed to be able to adapt to whatever concerning situation surfaced. He did so with humor, old-fashioned Southern charm, and the ability to weave in fantastical comments. Things did not always go his way, and as this chapter illustrates, when they did not, Harry engaged in less charming responses.

Of the many individuals I met who had spent significant years in state institutions, Harry appeared the happiest to be living in his community, with the front porch and the nearby park being two places he frequented almost daily. Given his small stature and the numerous challenges presented to him, I learned a great deal about being adaptive from Harry.

When I talk about the silent, I do not mean to suggest that all of the people who graced my professional life were nonverbal or nonvocal. Harry was one of those individuals who talked ... a lot. In his late 40s when we met at the group home, he had been diagnosed with schizophrenia and mental retardation (as his condition was called at the time).

By the time Harry was in the institution, tooth-pulling had evolved to only pulling out the front top and bottom teeth. I suppose this is what more humane treatment looked like in the era not too long ago, when the silent were sent away and isolated from the world around them. He was prone to self-injurious behavior where he would bite his hands and arms, and the protocol was tooth-pulling. Hence, Harry's teeth were pulled.

Harry was small, about 5-foot-3, and only weighed about 130 pounds when we met that summer in the mid-1990s. He was slightly bow-legged, with brown floppy hair and olive skin. His stride was short and his gait unsteady. Harry always gave the appearance of being on the verge of falling down (and, in reality, this was something that did happen fairly regularly).

Harry wore jeans, a shirt, and a winter coat—which he called his "smoking jacket"—almost every day, rain or shine. Whether in the cold of winter or the heat of summer, Harry always donned his coat. Attempts to convince him not to wear it were usually met with a strong, "Hell, no."

Harry did not just talk a lot: He also cursed a lot. With a strong, slow, Southern drawl, he turned profanity into an art form, and those of us who questioned his fashion choices bore the brunt of his explicit word choices. He enjoyed walks in the park, listening to country music, the taste of soda pop, and wieners in any form, such as hot dogs and Vienna sausages. Aside from a distant family member with whom I had only peripheral contact, Harry was the first person I knew with schizophrenia. He had also been diagnosed with intellectual impairment and a seizure disorder.

For the most part, Harry was silly and fun to be around. His gap-toothed smile flashed as he went through his day. Staff were vigilant in which way they faced, as he made a habit of pinching a person's behind if their back was to him. "I'm a goosin' ya!" he would say loudly, while laughing unresponsively to redirections or admonishments to keep his hands to himself. If music was playing, he often danced to it. He liked to laugh, and his laugh was often accompanied by his broken-up narration of what he was laughing at. "That boy looks so silliness in that shirt," he would say, with his propensity to add "ness" to the end of many words.

When he was happy, he would talk about his favorite things: "Oh, that's so funniness. We are gonna get so many gooderness soda pops, and I'm a gonna get me a hamburger, and my mom and Aunt Thelma will be singin' and laughingness."

Harry was labeled as schizophrenic in large part because he suffered from *command hallucinations*, auditory hallucinations that tell the person to act in a certain way: a frightening private hell for a fairly gentle soul. Periodically, Harry would stare into the corner of the room and then get a look of deep worry on his face. He would scream in terror and yell at the apparitions that appeared. "Oh, those biggerness girls and Dr. Perry are in the corner shootin' glass in my eye! They want to kill me!"

He would start crying, ball his fist, and start hitting himself mercilessly in the head or biting his arm or hand. Any attempt to block him or reassure him that things were OK was ignored. With his lack of balance, he often sat down when these episodes began (thankfully). As they wound down, Harry often went through an end-of-episode ritual: He would take his hand, twirl it around in a circular, counterclockwise motion then swing his fist, palm side up, toward his head as if he were going to really knock himself for a loop. Fortunately, he rarely made contact with his head. The most common result was that he would fall back into his chair, where he would often rest for several minutes. This series of events was always disturbing to see, no matter how many dozens of times it happened.

Those of us who worked with Harry always wondered what it was he saw. We surmised that the "biggerness girls" were nurses who had worked in the institution, that Dr. Perry had been the psychiatrist, and that having "glass shot in my [his] eyes" may have been some physiological response to an as-needed medication. In psychiatric settings, problem behavior and emotional outbursts sometimes resulted in an injection of medications, agents that often sedated the person and quelled the situation temporarily. I remember the group home manager coming to work one day with a grin. She let the staff know she was reviewing Harry's records and found a mention of a Dr. Perry from Harry's days living in the institution. We were right—which may have been dumb luck or clever deduction—or a little of both.

Harry was the only person I ever worked with who had positive hallucinations. By this, I mean that some of the things he saw were not fear-inducing; rather, they seemed to bring him joy. These deliria seemed to occur more often on sunny days, when Harry was enjoying time on the front porch of the group home. He would make this unusual gesture with both of his hands, where his middle finger and pinky might be extended and then the other fingers on his hand would be slightly bent. He would raise his hands above his head and say "Look! There's Aunt Thelma and my mom. They look so prettiness. And there's Jesus, and they're comin' to bring me 10 cans of soda pop and 6 cans of wieners." He would laugh and then often attempt to tickle and goose people, elated at the visions he had just seen.

There were times Harry claimed to be seeing things that were not there and that were not truly episodes. These occurred especially often when it was his turn to help clean up after meals. For the residents who moved from an institution where they had been fed and clothed without active treatment, there were challenges of living in the community in a group home. The home placed a greater emphasis on independence, house upkeep, and responsibilities.

A staff member might review the schedule and say, "Harry, it's your turn to clear the table." From the dining room, we would hear, "I can't. My legs are broken." When we would check on Harry and assure him his legs were fine, he might say, "The voices are telling me not to clean, they are." When we redirected Harry, unmoved by his attempt to avoid his duty, he would say things like, "You sumnabitches are tryin' to kill me." If his claims were ignored, he would often blame his housemate, Robert, for some random offense.

Robert lived with Harry for decades in the institution, and they seemed to enjoy each other's presence ... until Harry was asked to do chores. When irritated, he called Robert by the nickname he had given him, "Poopoo." When the statement of voices commanding him to refuse his chores failed to provide relief from responsibility, Harry might point to Robert and say, "Goddamn Poopoo made the biggerness mess in here!" Following what were typically several redirections, Harry would let out a loud audible sigh and begrudgingly begin the task at hand, typically leaving us with, "You assholes always make me do all the work around here, you do."

Somewhere during his time in the institution, Harry had been offered cigarettes, a habit he continued and in which he happily indulged. Due to his minimal funds and health considerations, Harry's cigarettes were rationed. When it was time to smoke, Harry would go out to the porch. Because of his tremoring hands, he could not light the cigarette himself, so staff provided assistance. When he smoked, Harry would consume the cigarette in a single drag. We made sure Harry was sitting down as the rapid intake of the entire cigarette produced a temporary euphoria and left a buzz plastered across Harry's smiling face.

Due to his seizure disorder and the medication he took to keep them at bay, Harry was on limited fluid intake. To the best of my recollection, he could have 8 ounces per hour. For any grown man—but especially one with a propensity to believe others were, at times, attempting to do him harm—this did not go over well. After Harry had a drink, he would often immediately ask for another, "I'm still thirsty, goddammit, and you need to get me a drink."

We would gently explain the rules and redirect Harry, as we had been trained. Explanations of the doctor's orders were always given and were always met with something to the effect of, "Well, he's a real asshole and he hates me! He wants me to die! Well, I'll show him and I'm just going to break my head open." Thankfully, Harry's deliberate attempts at self-harm were similar to his self-injurious episodes at the end of his hallucinations: He would take time to set up attempting to hit himself, but the production, more often than not, produced no harm.

Trying to help the residents experience a normal existence of living in and being part of a community did present its challenges. Outings to local parks, shopping centers, and recreational sites or other activities were a regular part of the weekly schedule. The agency's attempts to integrate the residents into their neighborhoods and their surrounding environments were noble efforts. However, they were efforts that did not always work out as planned.

One hot summer day, a confluence of events led to an incident with Harry. The group home residents were scheduled to go to a local amusement park, and Harry indicated he would like to go. At the time of this particular outing, Harry was several weeks into recovery from a broken leg that was the result of falling down some steps at the home. Before the drive to the amusement park, Harry enjoyed a cold soda.

Shortly after we arrived, he asked for a drink, to which I replied, "Harry, we had a drink before we left, so it's going to have to be another 30 to 40 minutes. But we can go get an ice cream or some fruit."

"I don't want any of that stuff. I want a soda pop!" he said firmly and bluntly.

I reiterated, "Harry, we can get some ice cream or some fruit."

Harry noticed some soda machines, walked over to them, and, with his cast on his leg, sat down on a curb, folded his arms on his knees, and buried his head into his hands for several minutes. The day was sweltering, with temperatures in the 90s. After sitting like this in the hot sun for what seemed like an eternity, but was probably no more than 5 minutes, Harry picked his head up, pointed a finger at me, and said, "Listen, asshole, you need to get me a soda pop!"

While he may have thought his hardline stance would sway me, I replied, "Harry, I can't get your soda pop right now. We can get a drink in a little while, but until then we could get something cool like ice cream."

At that moment, a family was walking by. Harry shared this injustice with them by yelling, "This asshole won't get me no soda pop!" Slightly embarrassed, I tried to redirect him away, thinking things could not get worse.

"Listen, you asshole," Harry said. "If you're not gonna get me no soda pop, I'm gonna break my leg again."

He raised his casted foot just a few inches up in the air, and with his tongue out of his mouth to the side, he attempted to strike the foot down on the ground. Luckily, there was barely any force, so no damage was done. When the first attempt was unsuccessful, he tried again and again, becoming more and more irritated with each failed attempt. Harry was showing no response to redirection, was continuing to be agitated, and had begun to periodically bite his arm, so I told him we were going to have to leave. This increased the frequency and intensity of the self-biting.

With the heat blazing down on us, the existing broken leg, and the ongoing behavior episode, this day at the amusement park had to come to an end. I assisted Harry up on his feet while he cursed at me repeatedly. Robert and his aide accompanied us. Robert was visibly agitated at having to leave, to the point that he began biting his own hand. It seemed as if the afternoon would never end.

As the air conditioning cooled down the car and we started making our way back to the home, Harry and Robert both calmed down. The drive and the return to the comfort of home provided us all with a respite from the chaos of the amusement park.

I never remember laughing at these situations in the moment, but as I have gotten older, I smile and laugh thinking about the absurdity of being cursed at and screamed at over a soda. Although at that time I didn't find it particularly amusing, I did not take any of Harry's actions personally. I miss trying to help people overcome the big daily challenges of life.

Harry passed away a few years ago. I miss his gravelly voice, mannerisms, and gap-toothed smile. I do think he enjoyed living in the group home, having his own space with a recliner in his room, a swing on the front porch, and close proximity to the park. With his medical and psychiatric conditions, I saw the detriment created and problems that arise when choices are limited. Due to his medications, he could not drink when he wanted to drink. Due to his challenges with self-management and minimal funds, he could not smoke when he wanted to smoke.

With more limited choice making, I always thought that it was important for Harry to exercise his right to make certain decisions, even if they were ones I would not have chosen for him. He chose to smoke. He chose to wear his winter coat all year round. He could choose who would accompany him on walks. He would say, "I want Poopoo to go on a walk with me, but not the boy upstairs (Silas)." Harry had many struggles, but he managed them to the best of his abilities. I relish the times I spent with such a character.

CHAPTER 4

Robert

I use the term "the silent" intentionally, not because every individual in the book was literally silent—quite the opposite, some spoke well, and some said things we wish they hadn't said. I use the silent because, to me, it describes the fact that, for decades—if not hundreds or thousands of years—individuals afflicted with different types of conditions have been marginalized and separated from society. Silencing can come from being born without a voice. Silencing can also happen if you're locked away in an institution without family and advocates who will fight to make sure your rights are protected, as Robert was. Silence can happen if you are not able to live a full life due to chemical sedation and restraint. Silence is a respectful term—as it is what the person is being, not who the person is.

As I have continued to learn more about the complexities of what it is to be human, one truth I hold close is that there is great beauty in simplicity. Robert's life was uncomplicated, his primary focus always on what was transpiring in his immediate environment. The gift of verbal behavior enables learning without direct experience, the joy of reading, and talking with others. But this gift is also a curse, because it comes with the possibility of deceit, bias, and noise. When the noise is hushed, we attend to the moment more, argue less, focus on what we feel (whether emotionally or in a tactile sense), and enjoy just *being*.

I do not know if I have ever met someone who enjoyed daily routines and just being more than Robert. What was mundane to others was comforting to him. The act of sitting quietly and rocking seemed to provide him with great satisfaction. Robert was beautiful. His life was simple. I thank him for imparting his wisdom to me.

• • •

"Institutional" is more often a word said about places that largely only exist in movies, books, old photographs, and other chronicles of history. Wallbrook, the fictional Cincinnati-area institution featured in the movie *Rain Man*, is a beautiful brick building, well-staffed with kind, understanding professionals and competent doctors. The compassionate care seen in this movie is idyllic, hardly the reality for many of the silent. Now there are few people who live in institutions, and their numbers are dwindling as they pass on quietly. The institutions where they spent decades are increasingly shuttered, their walls holding memories and secrets of days gone by.

Like Artie, Robert had spent decades living in an institution. Robert had autism and was said to be nonverbal, and he was separated from society while not yet an adult. He had moved into the group home when it opened, accompanied by Harry, who was close in age and who lived with Robert for years in the institution. Like many of us, Robert liked his routines. He regularly woke up on his own and dressed himself for the day. His preference for clothing was jeans, a T-shirt, sneakers, and a sweatshirt, which he wore regardless of the weather.

Robert was a large man, about 5-foot-9 and 240 pounds, with large hands and feet. He walked heavily. He breathed heavily. Robert, also in his late 40s when we met in the mid-1990s, was balding, and as with Harry, he was missing his front top and bottom teeth as he was prone to biting himself. When he came across new staff or demanding situations, he would often bite his hand or wrist area. As a humanist, I view the standard institutional practice of removing the front teeth of those who were biters as cruel and unusual. As a behaviorist, it always bothered me since the action of putting mouth to hand or wrist never stopped for Robert. He continued to do it, even though the absence of his front teeth meant there was little chance of harming himself. No one ever changed his action, taught him something new, or enhanced his communication skills. They took away his teeth but did not solve the problem.

Because he did not communicate through speech, Robert would not have been able to protest having his teeth pulled, and there was no one there to say "Hold on. There's no way you are going to do this to him!"

Robert would, more often than not, point to the things he wanted. Following the times when he bit himself (we called it *self-biting*), he would often rub the area on his hand, pucker his lips, and gently kiss it. Robert enjoyed sitting and rocking on his porch swing, walking along the treelined gravel trail at the local park, and sitting with his roommates in the living room.

Seeing was not easy for Robert. His physicians suggested he had impaired vision. He would often bring objects close to his eyes, whether it was his lunch food, his clothing to look for a tag to figure out front from back, or his toothbrush to ensure the toothpaste was on the bristles.

Those of us who worked with Robert often discussed how he seemed to rely more on what he could hear. From all observations, Robert heard particularly well. He could easily understand simple directions and always seemed to enjoy the staff who worked one-on-one with him. Another by-product of his institutionalization was how Robert responded to what people said to him. He seemed to despise questions, preferring to be sternly directed instead. If a staff member said, "Robert, would you please change your clothes?" he would stomp his foot, bite his arm, and make a low-toned groan expressing his displeasure. If the staff member said, "Robert, go change," he would walk upstairs on his own, go to his bedroom, and change his clothes.

As a young professional still learning the basics of psychology and ABA, I had no idea how to help him in this regard. While my colleagues and I were kind to this big, gentle soul, we simply resorted to providing directives kindly and firmly, as it did not cause him upset.

With his sensitivities to particular patterns of how others spoke to him, Robert would often respond to new staff members with wrath. It was as if he could sense the rookies right away, and the veterans would stand back and watch Robert work on them the way he had worked on all of us on our first days with him. New staff at the agency did receive some training, but nothing makes up for the need to *pair*, to spend time with someone developing a relationship. Robert would begin the morning by taking a seat on the couch dressed in his customary jeans, T-shirt, sweatshirt, and sneakers. And then the "fun" would begin.

When new staff spoke to him, he would often get up and walk to his room, pounding the stairs with his weighty steps. Then, when he left his room, he would descend slowly, often stopping halfway down the stairs. He would be wearing his typical daily attire, with certain fashionable changes, like a pair of underwear over his jeans, or a second or third sweatshirt on top of his correctly placed sweatshirt with only with his head through the neck hole. He might come down the stairs and parade himself in front of the new staff. Any direction given would result in deep grunts of disagreement as Robert made his way up to his room, only to come down a few minutes later with only a single arm in his sweatshirt and an extra pair of underwear pulled over only one knee on top of his jeans. It was a predictable, hilarious initiation ritual, and making it through this tribulation was typically followed by brighter days for Robert's staff.

Robert's life at the group home was seemingly a good life. It was a simple life. He seemed to relish the day-to-day: the food served, his daily showers, walks, and running errands with the staff and his housemates. For Robert, fixing meals at home was a vast improvement from food served on a tray; a shower and shave were probably better enjoyed in private versus sharing a communal bathroom; and the activities of a normal home life were superior in quality, number, and diversity than the planned activities of a unit.

On a difficult day for one of his housemates at a local amusement park, I remember how much fun Robert had walking around, enjoying the hustle and bustle of the rides, games, and attractions. I often wondered how different his life was now from what it had been. I wished he could tell us the stories, but then again, it may be better that we didn't know anything beyond what we knew from observing his daily enjoyment and smiles. Maybe that was just enough.

SECTION 2

The Silent in a Dangerous World

The silent are vulnerable. The most obvious vulnerability is the inability to speak or having difficulty speaking. How do you say "yes" or "no?" How do you state how you feel? How do you report being treated nicely, unfairly, or inhumanely? People are silenced in many ways including not being able to speak, being able to use a communication device but not having it present, living behind locked doors and locked walls, being chemically sedated, or having others speak for them who do not represent them or their perspective. The silent are so vulnerable that the behavior analysts serving this population formed a certification body, the Behavior Analyst Certification Board® (BACB®). Some pursued licensure to increase professional oversight and offer greater protection to the silent.

The silent face a real, ever-present danger from others. These are strange times, where reading and science are devalued and charlatans decry science and condemn the critical use of vaccines. This denial of the value of vaccines poses a real danger. One of the first targets of the anti-vaccination swindlers was the autism community. We are in an age where misinformation, propaganda, speculation, and pseudoscience compromise the lives of the silent and society at large. Unfortunately, these frauds do not appear wearing all black, with obviously divisive lectures or speeches. Instead, they appear with degrees, credentials, alluring words, wide open arms, smiles, and false promises. I worked with a family where both parents had given up their professions in Europe and moved to the United States when a crackpot physician promised that his expensive, unfounded treatment would produce speech for their nonvocal son. Thousands of dollars later, with their lives torn asunder and their silent son still silent, they came to me seeking the same promise, one I could not give them. The swindlers are there, ready to prey on those most desperate for assistance: the suffering, the afflicted, and the hopeless.

Across the last three decades, I have noticed trends: Every 5 to 10 years, some self-professed experts begin touting new treatments. These novel approaches are *never* grounded in the principles of science but in the false promises of tapping into hidden abilities, reaching people on a different level, and quickly resulting in nothing less than miraculous progress. Miracles don't come easy. The miracles of the silent are not found in such grand displays but in their perseverance, the small victories that are hard to see if you are not looking, and the joy they take in the things we take for granted. Simple milestones are miracles and probably should be celebrated as such. The snake oil salesmen preying on the silent and their families sell a bill of goods they cannot deliver, appealing to hope and love, and seizing upon desperation. For example, true believers of facilitated communication (FC) avoid empirical tests.

When the more guarded express their skepticism, these frauds claim the silent "don't feel the need to prove themselves," "have test anxiety," and "don't trust the evaluators." A series of excuses is used by those peddling such "therapies" to avoid scientific tests to prove or disprove the veracity of their claims. Their behavior allows for the continued exploitation of the silent and their families.

My own shift to a more scientific worldview came gradually. I remember hearing stories about "miracles" and "breakthroughs" in autism circles. Glossy, two-minute clips about autism discoveries covered by journalists intent on a scoop gained headlines and sparked curiosity. These "breakthrough" approaches rarely, if ever, produced tangible results. With each new perspective and treatment, many caregivers bought in both psychologically and financially, seeking the definitive cause, cure, or treatment. The proponents of these "latest and greatest" interventions asked families to believe, have faith in the treatment, and invest their time and money—and then gauge the "progress" resulting from the "intervention" subjectively.

I consider FC (now rebranded as "assisted typing" and associated with the "rapid prompting" method) as the most damning of the many fraudulent fads that dominated this time period. Posited as a key to unlocking the latent abilities of those with autism, it was quickly adopted by masses of caregivers longing to communicate with their children.

The stories of Jed and Dan are cautionary tales against the adoption of fad treatments. Their silence was made more challenging by their manipulation. I felt for them at the time and am happy the fraudulent treatment to which they were exposed is no longer part of their daily lives.

CHAPTER 5

Jed

Being human means we have, with a little help, the abilities to overcome and redefine ourselves. Jed was, in every way, a success story, a person who surmounted difficult circumstances to become a healthier, more well-rounded, independent version of himself. At the same time, he had to leave his home and community to get the help he needed. Advances in medicine, diagnoses, awareness, and behavioral science have not always been accompanied by increased availability of help and services.

Probably due to the significant gains he had made in life, some always believed there was "more" within him, something hidden and untapped. Rather than appreciate the colossal changes and valuing the smaller, slower successes that followed, some of his support team went down an all-too-familiar path: They turned away from the expertise of medicine and behavior science that had helped foster change and turned to pseudoscience. The only person adversely affected by this, of course, was Jed.

• • •

There was a saying popularized in the 1990s and applied to individuals with disabilities: "Not being able to talk is not the same as having nothing to say." A beautiful sentiment, it reminded the world to respect the silent. The saying was, unfortunately, hijacked by people supporting facilitated communication (FC), which is a fraudulent technique for providing "emotional support." The role of the facilitator in FC is to provide support by holding a person at the hand area as the person sits in front of a typing device. Through this physical assistance, this supposed stabilization of the hand allows the person being "helped" to produce typed messages.

With FC touted as a breakthrough that could unlock innermost thoughts and untapped potential, caregivers and professionals jumped at this easy way to reach the unreachable. Individuals who had never displayed much academic aptitude, who were not known to read or write, could all of a sudden do so fluently, artfully, and scholarly. Individuals with autism were reportedly writing sentences, paragraphs, songs, sonnets, and stories. They talked openly about being trapped within their bodies and about their autism. The writings suggested they knew the term autism, what it meant, and its implications. FC received media coverage that loudly trumpeted it as the means to tap into hidden potentials. Autism, it seemed, was not a complicated condition but an issue of apraxia. The FC technique was the key to unlocking autism's mysteries. This "therapy" caught hold like wildfire in the late 1980s and early 1990s, when it was covered in the media and espoused by its proponents as a revolutionary therapeutic intervention.

It seemed too good to be true.

It was.

Academics began designing studies to evaluate and understand FC. The findings in study after study pulled the veil back from this technique and demonstrated it was not the individuals with autism producing the typed messages but the facilitator holding their hand (Green, 1994; Montee et al., 1995; Wheeler et al., 1993). The facilitators were knowingly or unknowingly guiding the person's hand. Whatever hope was offered was replaced by the understanding that not only was FC unscientific, but some of its champions were also deceitful.

Jed was in his mid-20s in the mid-1990s and of average height and weight. He had not always been. Prior to moving to his group home, he was overweight due to inactivity at his home in a rural part of his home state. He was loud, large, and prone to very disruptive and aggressive actions. With little help available to them in the rural area they called home, Jed's parents contacted the agency to begin the process of having him relocate to a larger city, where he would be able to live and receive necessary services.

Upon moving to his new home and having regular daily activities established, Jed lost over 100 pounds. He communicated mostly by pointing and would periodically make one- or two-word vocal utterances. For example, if he wanted someone out of his personal space, he would say, "Bye-bye" as he waved. Jed sported a mustache, enjoyed car rides with music, walks in the park, and working on puzzles. He was learning to navigate the world around him as a healthy adult and mastering routines to build his growing independence, all *without* using any form of FC.

One summer, the agency that provided housing services for Jed invited an FC advocate to our town. Hailing from Australia, with dark silver-toned hair, a fair complexion, and a quick smile, Olivia arrived into town with quite an agenda: a tour of the various group homes, a keynote address at a local conference, and completing FC evaluations with residents with autism. Jed was one of the many clients selected for evaluation.

At this time, the company had offices on the 9th floor of an older office building. Built in 1926, it had no central air conditioning. This summer was particularly memorable for the oppressive heat plaguing the city, with temperatures in the mid- to high 90s.

As the assistant group home manager, I was asked to attend Jed's evaluation along with several others. The agency office had a small evaluation room with a similar-sized observation room, each maybe 8 feet by 8 feet. The evaluation and observation rooms were separated by a one-way mirror. It had been decided that the evaluation sessions would be videotaped. Without central air conditioning, the option to keep the room cool was to use the window unit. However, the unit was so loud that it compromised the sound of the video, so the powers that be decided to turn off the air conditioning for these sessions.

In the middle of a sweltering afternoon, I accompanied Jed to the 9th floor for his evaluation session. With a small table and chairs, only the facilitator, Olivia; Jed; and the group home manager, Molly, could fit comfortably in the evaluation room. Billy, a program director; Nick, a group home manager; our company CEO; and I were in the tiny observation room.

We knocked on the window to indicate the videotape was recording, and the session began. Standing on Jed's left side, Olivia grabbed his left hand to begin facilitation. Molly stood on Jed's right. As Jed "typed" with hand-held assistance, Olivia translated what Jed purportedly said. "How are you?" she would say. Jed, who had shown little to no interest in nor propensity for typing, would begin "typing," and Olivia would say, "Oh, he says he's doing very well today!"

I watched Jed. He seemed incredibly uncomfortable with the evaluation. He pressed his right hand firmly against his ear and began speaking softly. "Go, bye-bye," he repeated as he pointed to the door. As the minutes and the "facilitation" dragged on, Jed repeated, "Outside ... go outside." His pleas were ignored. Molly stood by silently as Olivia continued her evaluation. The room simmered, and the evaluation continued until Jed finally decided it was over: He reached his hand up and grabbed Olivia's hair, pulling her down violently.

Molly moved quickly but was unable to release Jed's grip. Olivia was bent over, remaining calm during this chaotic moment. Billy and I rushed to the door to get into the room to assist, but the door was locked from the inside! In what seemed like forever but was likely under a minute, we were finally able to get in and assist in releasing Jed's grip. Jed calmed down but repeated the same desire: "Outside." Billy and I stood close by. Molly was clearly flustered, her cheeks red and tears welling in her eyes. Olivia, to her credit, acted unfazed; stood up; brushed off her dark, wrinkled business suit; and ran her fingers through her graying hair.

After a few short moments, Olivia indicated it was time to recommence. Billy and I stood in the packed room in case another episode might transpire. In my head, I kept thinking, "Jed wants to go. He is doing and saying everything he can to get out of here. It is sweltering hot, stuffy, and he is in a small room with a complete stranger being asked questions while having his hand held as if he is an infant." My mind was racing, thinking another aggressive episode could happen at any moment.

Within just a few minutes, Olivia wound down the session and addressed Jed: "Is there anything you need to say, Jed?" Leaning over, Olivia led his hand to different keys on the device. She stood up, read his message, and smiled broadly, announcing to us, "Oh, he said he's sorry!"

Of course he did.

As Jed, Molly, and I began to exit, I overheard one of our company leaders say, "We really need to ramp up our efforts with this [FC]."

I could not believe what I was hearing. My heart sank, as I had feared the agency would begin facilitating with many of the clients whose stories appear in this book. Fortunately, some of my colleagues who were there pointed to the studies and testimonials demonstrating the absence of any evidence supporting FC as a legitimate intervention.

This scenario had lasting implications in shaping my skepticism for gimmicky "therapies" and reinforcing my appreciation for science and research. The explosion in the popularity of something does not make it valid. FC in its many incarnations and repackaging as a breakthrough treatment is an unproven treatment. We had a man doing everything he knew to do to remove himself from an uncomfortable situation. Rather than having his observable, specific communicative efforts acknowledged, Jed was ignored in favor of a flawed, now-discredited method being performed by an "expert," an authority.

In the midst of the attempt to showcase how this method afforded Jed and those like him opportunities to communicate, his real, observable, exact words were ignored, and his dignity compromised—all to demonstrate a pseudoscientific technique that has been discredited. Not being able to speak is, indeed, not the same as having nothing to say. But saying something, using your voice and having it ignored to the point where you lash out aggressively, should give anyone pause.

CHAPTER 6

Dan

Dan was a gentle man. Of the people featured in this book, Dan was among the most mellow. Observations suggested he enjoyed watching basketball and taking brisk walks in the park, and car rides. Dan needed help with most of his daily living skills, except for eating. Due to his history of classmates and housemates with more advanced skills and his propensity to acquire skills slowly, Dan's team was always looking for the means to motivate him and strengthen his skill sets.

Unfortunately, as with Jed, Dan's family was frustrated with his slow progress and latched on to the supposed breakthrough of facilitated communication (FC). When it failed to produce any noticeable gains, those who cared for him daily were asked to not trust their eyes and ears. His story reminds us of the perils of adopting non-evidence-based procedures.

• • •

Communication deficits are often part of what defines the silent. Myriad descriptive terms have been employed to describe the inability to communicate fluidly. Unfortunately, using descriptive terms tends to lead to a description not of the concern but of the people: "dumb," "nonverbal," "impaired," and "low functioning." Words matter, and using the wrong words has left in its wake characterizations the silent have never deserved. Aside from being labeled with prejudicial terms, the silent deal with much more pressing day-to-day, moment-to-moment issues that result directly from their difficulties with communication. Accessing reinforcers, describing illness or discomfort, saying "I love you"—none of it comes easily. This inability to communicate produces angst and worry for the silent and for their loved ones. Angst and worry breed desperation, and desperation sends us searching for anything and anyone who promises change—regardless of the impracticality of delivering impossible promises.

In the group home, Dan was the client with the most limited communication and leisure repertoire (the most behaviorally intensive client). He was in his late 20s during the mid-1990s, when our lives intersected. He moved with a slow, casual gait and often seemed to be preoccupied with his own actions. Dan did not attempt to speak, echo, or babble. He would periodically lead you by the hand or push something away that he didn't want. He made little eye contact and required assistance to complete most daily tasks and chores.

Dan was part of an involved, loving family, and his parents and younger brother visited often, smiled often, and were affectionate. They were educated, had a deep religious faith, and were involved in the local autism community. Despite the abiding love the family had, despite their optimism and dedication, Dan was more significantly affected and made slower progress than his housemates.

Dan was a gentle man who had few problem behaviors. He was in perpetual motion, pacing the halls of his home and enthusiastically walking local parks in the community. He appeared to like to move. The one problem behavior he did exhibit was not dangerous, but it was incredibly disruptive. Often when asked to remain still for any period of time for activities such as trimming his nails or performing other hygiene activities, Dan would emit a piercing scream (a shriek I've yet to hear equaled in sharpness, duration, and volume). His shrieks seemed to happen most often when he was asked to engage in certain demands, specifically those things that required him to be still or those that involved physical prompting.

Most daily activities for Dan required physical assistance, and staff learned to be gentle and give periodic breaks to minimize the likelihood of the soul-shattering scream. When Dan chose to sit down, he would cross one leg over the other and put his two index fingers to his eyes and make them squint. He appeared to be a man in deep in thought.

Dan had a major role in my remaining skeptical of the fad "fixes." As I continued to work with clients like Dan, there was a rash of "miracles" and "breakthroughs" in autism circles. FC, of course, was one of them. Dan's incredibly loving, kind, and supportive mother completely believed in the idea of FC. She had been told that by stabilizing her son's hand and providing (ill-defined) emotional support, she could assist him with typing on a device that would unlock his untapped inner mental potential and latent verbal abilities. These abilities were said to have been there all along, inside of Dan and other people with autism. It was purported that through the use of FC, the world could see into the thoughts and feelings of people who lacked vocal abilities, who rarely showed emotions, and whose affects were somewhat blunted. There was the suggestion that there was something more inside a person, something profound that could be revealed through this revolutionary technique.

With the belief that together they had tapped into Dan's hidden intellectual abilities through FC, his mother enrolled him in the local university to audit a history course. Dan and his mother would go to the class, armed with their keyboard. Dan did not make or hold eye contact. The university setting presented him with a challenging activity: the demand of having to sit for extended periods with dozens of other students present. Eventually, Dan would begin screaming. In the midst of this, his mother would still be holding his hand, typing messages about what "he" was learning. I was shocked that others missed the obvious—there is no way a person can scream while looking away from a device and still be able to type a coherent response.

This scenario had to be difficult for the other students and the professor, and I am certain there were times it caused suffering for Dan's mother. She would admonish Dan gently when the classroom visit didn't go well, and they would return to the group home early. Ultimately, it had to have been the most difficult for Dan, whose dearest and most ardent advocate was also the person making him sit still in an environment that was foreign, felt hostile, and was likely aversive (generally, a stimulus that produces avoidance behavior). As my time with Dan continued, I adopted a functional view of his behavior: His screaming may have been an indicator of annoyance and irritation and was his way of communicating that he did not want to be in that class or be in that environment.

Unfortunately, the use of FC with Dan continued even after this failure. During her weekly visits, Dan and his mother would "converse" through the typing device. Dan and his mother typed, and she would read his typed messages aloud and talk with him. By and large, Dan's mother would smile and laugh at the exchanges, and although I (and others) privately questioned the veracity of the messages, they *seemed* harmless at the time.

CHAPTER 6: DAN

Falsehoods and fraudulent treatments left unverified, though, can have unanticipated negative effects. Once, Dan's mother came to speak with me when I was serving as the assistant manager of the group home, and she claimed Dan had authored a message while typing with her. According to the message, on a Sunday at 9:30 a.m., a female staff member had become irritated because Dan had not wanted to take a shower and he had resisted by walking away and screaming. It was stated that she smacked his hand, not hard, but out of frustration with Dan's opposition.

Immediately, we began investigating. We were shocked at the seriousness of the allegation and perplexed, as the accused person was one of our kindest and most compassionate staff members. None of the staff had reported seeing the named female staff member hit him. There were no marks on Dan's hands. As we remained concerned and delved further, we looked through our records and found that not only had the accused female staff member not worked with Dan that day, but she had been off work the Friday, Saturday, and Sunday of that entire weekend in which the incident supposedly occurred. There was no truth to the claim.

For many of us working with Dan at this time, this incident solidified our viewpoints about the deceitful nature of FC and the inherent danger of allowing a person to have direct influence over typed messages attributed to another person. Dan had not typed the message by himself. He did not attempt to avoid this staff member. He did not engage in problematic behavior in this staff member's presence. There were no indirect or direct indicators of any problem. The message was fiction, an embellishment that could have been disastrous to the staff member had we not been more skeptical and investigated the matter thoroughly.

For Dan's mother, the explanation was different: Dan had wanted attention and made the story up to see what would happen.

She therefore reprimanded him about "lying" but continued making FC part of their weekly interactions.

Once adopted, fraudulent treatments can be very hard to let go, especially when they are based in a sincere and fervent hope for success mixed with encouragements by proponents of those treatments to believe in their success. If you have invested your time, belief, and money into something, you want to see those investments pay off. When someone who has never uttered a solitary spoken word types messages expressing sentiments of love, weaves a story of being trapped inside a body unable to find and say words, or recalls fond memories of family vacations, who wouldn't want to believe it?

Interventions, though, are not beliefs. They are methods that can be detailed, observed, measured, and tested. They do not require faith. FC is not a communication method but direct manipulation of one person's hand by another. After having undergone rigorous scientific evaluation, FC should have been eliminated as a therapeutic technique. Just like leeching, exorcisms, and magic elixirs, FC as currently practiced should take its place in the pantheon of ineffective, unnecessary treatments.

Unfortunately, FC remains in use and has been rebranded and repackaged under different names. It provides a false promise of hope that delivers to the facilitator the types of messages they desire or expect to see. The approach has not been validated by evidence but by anecdote, so it continues its decades-long deceit of preying upon the helpless.

For me, the wonder of interacting with the silent has never been about finding a miraculous cause and cure. The joy I found was in the dignity they displayed amid the struggles and the tiny surprises, idiosyncrasies, and small discoveries. This dignity made me like them even more.

CHAPTER 6: DAN

Every weekend, I hoped to be assigned to work with Dan. We bonded through basketball, a sport my brothers, father, and grandfather all played. In the part of the country where Dan lived, basketball was the most popular sport and an important part of the societal fabric.

Dan's brother attended a university where basketball was nearly a religion, with the games being broadcast on TV on Saturdays or Sundays. Dan was the only resident with a TV in his room. Around noon on the weekends, Dan would often go to his room and approach the TV, something he never did on weekdays. He would turn on the TV and then turn the channel knob through the various TV stations until he found the basketball game.

Dan would sit back in his recliner, typically crossing his left leg over his right and putting both of his index fingers to the corners of his eyes, and watch the entirety of the basketball game. I never saw Dan cheer for the team, nor did he appear upset if the team lost, but he sat still, often smiling throughout the game.

To this day, I don't know how Dan learned this repertoire. For a young man who wrestled with independence, who found making choices difficult, and whose communication was arduous, he was often able to locate his brother's university basketball games on TV at the appropriate time and watch them as if he were sitting in his home with his family. It was a beautiful thing: Amid his challenges, Dan had the most clearly identified interest of any of the residents and the most independent repertoire in accessing this interest.

I wish I could explain how it all worked. I cannot. But I hold onto these memories of good times spent with someone with my shared passion for basketball. Whatever communication complications existed were overcome for a few hours by the joy of being in proximity with another person sharing a common pastime.

SECTION 3
The Richness of Life Well Lived

The eminent psychologist B. F. Skinner advocated that when we find something interesting, we should stop everything we are doing and study it. That is the job of a behavioral scientist. That is what fascinated me about the silent (and still does): Whatever programs were written, schedules made, or ideas hatched, something could happen at any time, and we can carefully examine the things that happened before and after the behavior and attempt to rearrange the environment so the problem behavior won't happen again.

Behavior science puts an emphasis on teaching people skills. It equipped me with the ability to observe and collect data and showed me that each day offered new opportunities to teach skills. I found the calling to serve as a behavior analyst to be nothing short of magical.

Telling these stories is a wonderful form of free therapy. I have dipped back into memories of some of the best times of my life. Challenges occurred, but the bulk of the time I spent with the silent was enjoyable. We laughed. We learned. We lived life—walking, talking, listening to music, and visiting places they had never seen. There were simple moments of joy at meals, birthdays, and holidays. There was the repetition of teaching daily living skills. There was the awareness that some of these people who had been locked away from the world were now free to live in homes and nice communities. This awareness was balanced by the reality that, for some of the people described here, their needs demanded specialized services and support that could only be found in tightly controlled environments.

Wherever the silent live, though, we need to maximize our time with them. Time with most clients, however, is temporary and fleeting. We enter into the lives of the silent as they enter into ours, with responsibilities and goals and promises of hope and better days yet to come. Human services are just that: *human*. We are inevitably reinforced by many of the things that happen within these shared relationships. Psychoanalysts warn therapists about defense mechanisms while behavior analysts caution about dual relationships. The idea is the same: When we get to know people better, when we assist them through difficult times, and when we bear witness to progress (even in its smallest form), those shared experiences may come to closely resemble familial bonds and friendship.

Our clients come to care about us, and we come to care about them. It is a challenge to separate what we are experiencing personally from what we are experiencing professionally. Several of the people featured in the book (and many of the people with whom I have worked) were wards of the state. They may have had an appointed case manager or guardian representing them, but who would be there for birthdays? Surgeries? Dances? Holidays? I prided myself in being there for them.

There are important discussions about what constitutes professional boundaries. We should discuss what words to use and whether our professional and ethical codes properly address this complicated aspect of human service work. Ultimately, though, each word and action should be a reflection of acting selflessly in the other person's best interest, knowing that we are a small but important part of the person's environment.

The stories of JD, Silas, Heidi, and Joey reveal beautiful individuals challenged by circumstance and working earnestly to live full lives. When I think about them, I smile.

Working with the silent has been one of life's joys. I hope each person mentioned here—and the many whose stories have not been told —may one day know they have made me feel like the richest man on the face of the earth. I am so lucky the silent shared part of their worlds with me.

CHAPTER 7

JD

There are angels among us. They have no wings, and their deeds are far from heavenly. When you find yourself in their presence, though, or recall your times with them, you cannot help but be overwhelmed by a feeling of warmth. In the moment, or perhaps weeks, months, or years later, you catch yourself laughing at something they said or something you did together. The miracles they perform are not grand. They see the world differently and then share their insight with you. They react distinctly and allow you the joy of witnessing their uniqueness. The cynicism of the world escapes them, their attentions focus on the joys of the more mundane—and you know the world is a far better place because of them.

The few short years I worked with JD were distinguished by growth—both his and mine. As his school grades and social interactions improved, my knowledge of behavior analysis soared. With his increased social repertoires, I was cultivating a greater interest in how applied behavior analysis (ABA) could be used to help JD improve his abilities to interact with his peers: his personal, self-stated goal. With each idea I had, he offered me opportunities to explore it. We were an incredibly productive, happy team, and I was blessed to have been given the chance to learn from him. My world is far better because of my time with him.

• • •

JD and I were kindred spirits. When we first met, I was discovering ABA and the many promises it holds. JD was a short, thin, teenage boy with black hair and brown eyes who was beginning to be more involved in the world around him. JD was not silent; he spoke well and often, albeit in a very robotic manner. His every action helped me understand numerous aspects of human behavior. Among the many clients who have graced my life, he was my greatest teacher. At that point in my professional life, I was excited at the things I was reading and the techniques and programs I was developing, and I would discuss them with anyone willing to listen.

I arrived at JD's family home on the first day of working with him. The brick house sat on hill in a neighborhood close to a large cemetery. His parents welcomed me in and showed me to JD's room, where he was watching television attentively.

"Hi, JD. I'm Andrew. What are you watching?"

He looked right at me and in his staccato delivery said, "Hello, Andrew. *Jerry Springer: Trailer Park Queen.*"

One of the keys to being successful as a behavior analyst is to assess people's preferences. We all have preferences, and they tend to be the things that motivate us. It occurred to me that JD was expressing preferences, so I probed by asking,

"What are your top 10 TV shows?"

JD's eyes got big. (I had made a friend for life.) He listed from 10 to 1 every sensational TV show, from *Sally Jessy Raphael* to *Montel Williams* to *Inside Edition*. Each time we worked together, I would say, "What's today's top 10, JD?" Prior to answering, he would freeze, place his hand on his chin in a classic thinker pose, tilt his head upward, and then begin the process of listing out in reverse order his top 10. While the order changed, JD typically ranked *Jerry Springer* as his favorite show (much to the chagrin of his parents).

During our first meeting and most of the sessions that followed, JD often kept in his hand a gray device that looked like a video camera but was actually a cassette recorder-player. Holding it close to his ear, he would play a brief segment, then rewind and replay it again and again and again.

"What are you listening to?" I inquired.

Placing the device to my ear, JD pressed play.

"Duh-duh-duh-da-duh. KPIX! Channel 5, San Francisco."

My time with JD was filled with discovery and learning, including facts about TV stations, TV programming, TV news anchors and their bios, and local news.

JD had savant abilities. He memorized the online biographies of dozens of newscasters and could recall facts about where they went to school and their interests. You could give him a date, December 14, 1969, for example, and he could tell you that the day was Sunday. In years past, individuals with autism were sometimes referred to as "idiot savants," since some displayed uncanny, isolated abilities but still had trouble with self-help or social skills. I despise that term and am glad that it is no longer preferred, as it is considered denigrating to the person and trivializes their gifts and capabilities.

JD's gift was on full display when we went to the local mall to a store with compact discs and videos. After browsing through some CDs, JD held up a video cassette with the picture of a woman.

"Andrew, can I buy Pamela Anderson's *Playboy*® video?" JD asked.

Calmly, I replied, "Not today. You are only 14. You have to be 18 to buy *Playboy*."

JD walked a few steps away, suddenly turning around and hustling back.

"Andrew, in 1,233 days can I get Pamela Anderson's *Playboy* video?"

He had calculated the exact number of days until his 18th birthday.

I responded: "JD, when you are 18, you can make those decisions. Until then, put it back, please."

Teachers of behavior analysis often have learning labs. JD educated me on autism and ABA in the lab at the university library where we often worked. This was when computers were moving from monochrome to colored displays, and we were experiencing the advent of the internet. JD was good with computers and had an affinity for technology. He actually taught me how to access Netscape (one of the first web browsers) and opened my own world to the endless information of the web. One of the things I was told was that JD's grades were marginal, consisting of a few Bs and several Cs. As JD opened my eyes to technology, my adviser was having me pour over journals and books about ABA. The convergence of all of this was one discovery after another.

One of the methods used to foster behavior change is a *behavior contract*. A document is drawn up between the therapist and client stipulating mutual agreement about what behaviors can or cannot occur for a specific period of time, and should the contract be met, a reward will be delivered. JD and I entered into behavior contracts regularly. We had small contracts for upcoming assignments and tests, with JD often choosing computer time or a visit to the mall as his preferred activity. We had large contracts for grades, where JD would pick a TV station within a 2-hour drive that we could visit if he met the terms. JD loved the contracts, and they were remarkably effective, with his grades improving to all As and Bs. We would drive to various TV stations and get tours, and JD was even permitted to sit in the news anchors' chairs and take pictures at the news desks.

When particularly difficult assignments were due, I learned about the power of preference. JD enjoyed game shows. I would spend a few hours making hand-drawn game show boards with questions related to the topic of the upcoming assignment. The game show *Jeopardy!* was always a hit with him. When I would say, "The year the Declaration of Independence was signed," JD would smile, fold his hands dramatically as if he were on camera, look at me, and say, "What is 1776, Andrew?" "You're right, for $100," I responded, and he would throw his hands up victoriously. Learning with JD was fun, fast-paced, and a reminder to evaluate preferences to help build skills.

There were so many good times. This is not to say JD could not be difficult. He was a teenager, after all. When we first began our work together, JD was approaching friends at his public school where he was enrolled in the general education program. He would walk up and say, "WLOS, where is it?" If the peer could not answer correctly, he would perseverate, saying "You don't know! You don't know!" or "That's wrong. It is incorrect. That is bad!" Several things were gleaned from these events. First, JD was using TV call letters as a means to initiate social interaction, which suggested social interaction was becoming increasingly important to him. Second, he needed to learn how to cope when people were wrong, since most people do not have perfect recall of the call letters of TV stations.

In the same library where we spent so much of our time, I found a study by researchers Lynn McClannahan and Patricia Krantz on *script fading* (Krantz & McClannahan, 1993). This intervention involves writing out a phrase or sentence and then gradually reducing the size of the font, washing out the color, or removing letters. It is a technique utilized to gradually wean the person from the actual script. JD had strong reading skills, so we developed scripts, practiced, and reinforced more appropriate interactions. Through script fading, JD learned to approach his peers more effectively. For example, he would say, "Hi, Christi," wait for her reply, and then say, "Do you know where WLOS is?" If Christi said, "No," as JD's peers often did, he would say, "WLOS is in Asheville, North Carolina. Have a good day!"

Script fading was so effective that we even started recognizing JD's initiations as attempts to communicate more information. For example, if he asked about a local TV station, he began to follow up with what he did that weekend, like attending a basketball game with his father. If he asked about WLOS, he would let people know his grandmother lived in a town outside Asheville.

Then one day, the world—the world wide web really—came crashing down. After working for about an hour and completing homework, we walked over to the computers, as JD often selected them as his reinforcer. To our dismay, they were not working.

"Oh, no! Oh, no! This is bad! This is bad! They're not working!" JD yelled repeatedly.

"Do you know where we are, JD?" I asked.

"The library," he replied.

"Yes, and there's two things you need to know," I said.

"What's that?" he asked.

"First, it's the library so you have to be quiet. Second, libraries have lots of books and magazines, including *TV Guide*. Do you want to go find them?"

CHAPTER 7: JD

In the library stacks, we eventually found the back issues of *TV Guide*, a magazine listing television stations, program names, and broadcast times. Having observed JD paging through the *TV Guide* at home, I took a chance. JD had found the next best thing to being on a computer and would, in fact, sometimes choose reading the *TV Guide* as his activity.

A few years prior to my meeting JD and his family, his mother had been in a serious car accident. She suffered physical and brain injuries that would plague her until she died (sadly, only a few years later). The brain injuries likely made her impatient, curt, and truculent. Whatever social niceties she lacked, she probably had no control over the resultant damage the accident had done to her. And so, in the waning days of my time in graduate school, JD's mother made a demand: "I need you to take JD to summer camp."

At that time, JD and I were working together, as his social behaviors were the subject of my in-progress thesis. I was completing my last internship at a community mental health center and preparing for life beyond graduate school. JD's mother wanted me to take him to a weeklong camp on the other side of the state.

"I'm sorry. I cannot take him. I have my thesis and internship and have to finish both of them," I said.

"If you don't take him to camp, then I will pull him from your thesis and you won't graduate," she threatened.

"Completion of the thesis isn't required," I replied.

JD's mother made the decision about this camp and my involvement, and she had not told him about it. I was sorry to hear this ultimatum—sorry not just for me, but for JD.

I would never work with JD again.

The heartbreaking decision crushed me. JD was making progress. He and I had work left to do. Regardless of this premature separation, my time with JD was coming to an end soon as a result of my pending graduation. I had already planned to move back to Florida a month and a half after graduating. I accepted his mother's decision. I believe that had JD's mother's circumstances been different, she would never have acted the way she did, and my time with JD would never have come to such an abrupt end.

Several years later, a friend sent me a newspaper article from the local paper about JD as part of a series of articles for Autism Awareness Month. In their feature on JD was a picture of him in headphones at a microphone. He no longer looked like the teen I worked with. He was now a man and was hosting a weekly radio show where he played jazz music, gave news updates, and got to say call letters several times an hour.

I smile every time I think about JD and what he is doing now, happy for the mark he made in my life, teaching me all he did about autism, TV, and ABA.

CHAPTER 8

Silas

Awareness is a complicated idea. To our friends in psychology, awareness is about being able to perceive something, to be conscious. As a behaviorist, I do not observe from the same vantage point—a behaviorist does not consider consciousness and other mentalistic constructs and concepts such as personality, intelligence, and emotion in explaining a behavioral phenomenon. Instead, we look to the environment for what determines circumstances where one is aware or unaware. I wonder if we ever stop to think, whatever perspective we adopt, about whether any of us is always aware. In a time in life when I was exploring both psychological and behavioral views on a host of topics, Silas helped me understand awareness by how he moved through his life: periodically painfully aware of his life's circumstances, and at other times, blissfully unaware of what plagued him or how he was seen by others. Awareness for him was not a way of being; instead, it was a series of actions such as observing his own behavior, describing his personal history, or stating what made him unique. It was the times when this awareness troubled him, tore at him, and tortured him that I wished for an easy explanation and a simple solution. While I offered what support I could, I never found either.

Maybe that was the lesson. A behavior-analytic view looks directly at human action as the focus of study, the target for assessment and intervention. Nowhere in the data, the volumes of journals and textbooks, and the theories in books are the terms "easy" or "simple" typically used. Silas was complicated—as are all people—but I am grateful that the behavioral view I hold was always compatible with humanistic inclinations. I could honor and respect Silas (and my other clients) and preserve his dignity through some trying events while still insisting on data collection and analysis as the best means to try to understand complex behavioral phenomena.

• • •

Silas was a housemate of Harry and Robert. It would be nice to say they were friends. They were not. Whereas Harry and Robert had lived in a particular institution together, and Judith, the lone female resident, liked all of the housemates, Silas saw himself as quite different from them. Silas was conversational, energetic, and independent; had some reading ability; and was incredibly athletic. He was in his early 20s, while Harry and Robert were in their 40s. A towering 6-foot-3 and weighing 260 pounds, he was larger, more coordinated, and more advanced cognitively and socially than his housemates.

Silas lived in the lone room on the third floor. It was a very neat place for a young man who preferred his own space with his own staff. Silas's dressers were adorned with medals and trophies, the result of many athletic competitions and victories.

He kept his light brown hair very short and was inclined to wear athletic shorts and T-shirts, regardless of the temperature. It was rumored his disabilities were the result of horrific abuse during his childhood. While Silas had no family, several adults from his high school and the agency were particularly fond of him, so his holidays and birthdays were spent with caring and decent people who treated him like family.

Silas's favorite pastimes were collecting sports cards and sorting through them. A burgeoning reader, he loved to talk about his cards and the athletes, some of whom he recognized, and decipher some of the names, words, and facts on the cards. Whatever he could not read, staff would help him with. It was not an expensive collection, but it was priceless to him.

In my time working in group homes and residential treatment centers, the ability of the residents to have personal possessions was a luxury. Many times, personal items were lost, destroyed, or stolen, so they were exceptionally rare; and in many cases, family and caregivers were discouraged from providing them. The group home manager, Matilda, insisted Silas should have his collection and encouraged staff to help him tend to it.

Silas had gone to a high school in the same area as the home and loved the social aspects of that connection. A few years after graduating, he still talked regularly about his high school experiences. He was charming, and he frequently spoke with considerable confidence about liking girls and having girlfriends. Every few months, Silas went to dances held for adults with disabilities. Dressed in his gray suit and his gray dress shoes, he spent the evenings flirting and dancing with several young ladies.

He would come home with phone numbers from these young ladies and would have phone conversations with them. Sooner or later after these events, he would strike up a conversation about a woman—or more than one woman—being his girlfriend. Understandably, flirting with several women and having several numbers did not work out for him. In the small town where we lived, Silas sometimes flirted with young women who were classmates and friends. They would eventually find out about his multiple flirtations and interests and suspend any talk about being his girlfriend.

Silas relished time with group home staff and largely avoided community outings with his peers from the home. His social filter was not well developed, and he would sometimes utter profanities and say unkind things to his housemates such as, "I ain't like them. They can't even talk!"

On rare occasions, he would hurl direct insults, such as, "You are fucking retarded" or "Christi took me to Thanksgiving dinner while you guys just sat here." Judith would yell at him to "shut up," while Harry and Robert did not pay him much attention. Silas saw himself as very different from his housemates, but these outbursts were rare. He was mostly content to have the third floor to himself and to have permission to do things with his staff by himself.

Psychiatric services for Silas, and many of the other clients, puzzled me. I was young and new to clients taking medications. Silas's hands tremored when taking medications, and he had pronounced, albeit less frequent, *stereotypy*: repetitive, nonfunctional behaviors sometimes referred to as self-stimulatory behavior or loosely referred to as "stimming." All of the clients were on medications, and Silas was on some strong antipsychotic medications with horrendous side effects. We were told one of his medications made him highly susceptible to sunburn, and despite having some pigmentation, he did burn quickly when he was outside too long. If we went to doctor visits with the group home manager and there was any mention of an improvement in Silas's mood, before we could give any detail, the psychiatrist would change the medications. It seemed unprofessional because no further discussion was considered at all, despite the clear negative side effects of some of the medicines. I became more aware of the challenges of dealing with medicines and the silent when I had the privilege of working with two wonderful psychiatrists at the center a few years later.

The agency was keen on having residents spend time out in the community. Group home staff worked 8-hour shifts of 7:00 a.m.–3:00 p.m., 3:00 p.m.–11:00 p.m., and 11:00 p.m.–7:00 a.m. I preferred morning shifts on the weekends.

In working with Silas, one of the things you knew was that he would be up early. None of the clients in the group home slept in—not a single one of them. No matter how many medications they were on or what transpired the night before, the odds were your client was up, dressed, bathed, and teeth brushed—ready to go from the moment you arrived at 7:00 a.m. It was also a given that Silas would want to do community-based activities. He loved going to the mall, the park, a ballfield, or the local university.

For those wanting to help clients expand their communicative and social repertoires, having a client with Silas's energy and varied interests was a perk of the job. However, for anyone who had been out late the night before and arrived at 7:00 a.m. feeling the effects of too little sleep (this was a college town, after all), a shift with Silas would challenge their resolve. He was going to jog, shoot baskets (regardless of the cold), and want to drive somewhere in the community.

A left-handed, multisport athlete, Silas enjoyed training for and participating in Special Olympics events, watching sports on television, and attending sporting events at the local university. Silas's days were active, and he was fully immersed in chores and sports.

We spent many hours at the basketball hoop that hung over a storage shed in the backyard. Silas was the king of his home court, taking on all comers.

"No one can beat me. You're just not good enough," he would say.

For some context, I was a high school basketball player. This did not matter to Silas. When we competed, he always played hard. He would dribble the ball, cock it slightly off his left ear, and shoot toward the sky. When the ball went through the net, he would drop his shoulders, strut, look over at me (or whomever he was playing), and grin widely, shaking his head back and forth as he pursed his lips as if to say, "Ooh, no one can stop me."

These were fleeting but exciting moments, and sharing them highlighted the importance of engaging with clients in what they love to do. Who won—and it was usually Silas—was irrelevant. It was about sharing those simple moments. I didn't know it then, but I miss those simple times, and I am glad to have shared them with such an opponent.

Silas mowed the tiny group home yard with a manual push mower. He had more chores than his housemates, but part of doing the chores was an attempt to prepare him for outside employment. Unfortunately, it was challenging to obtain gainful employment for him. While more vocal and academically advanced than his housemates, Silas was prone to, as one staff member called it, "show out." Rarely aggressive and with no history of harming anyone, he had an imposing physical size, along with a tendency to make a fist, stare, hit walls and objects, and periodically make threats. He was once hired by a local fast-food establishment, but he lost his job when he punched the freezer door. No employer can retain employees who intimidate their coworkers, despite reassurances of a nonaggressive history.

Another time, Silas secured a job doing basic yard care. He only lasted a couple of weeks because he was sneaking his Jason mask (from the *Friday the 13th* movies) to work and wearing it while carrying sharp objects. While he never hurt anyone, he certainly did frighten them.

Although I never felt threatened by Silas, I did wonder if he ever did become really aggressive whether I could safely manage the situation. I was fairly confident in my abilities to de-escalate vocally, and I hoped I could safely manage a physical situation. Still, it was a relief that things never came to that.

Of the many individuals whom I encountered during my work, Silas may have been in the most difficult of predicaments: He was vocal enough and intelligent enough to realize, at times, that he was different. Despite his talents, athleticism, and skills, he was unable to do things others could do and was seen by people as being "special." Silas hated this, even if he could do little to mask his disabilities from others. At times, the frustration was visible: With his left leg forward, right foot back, and both arms bent, he would rock back and forth, often teetering forward within inches of others' faces.

What he could not hide sometimes embarrassed him and reminded him of his disabilities—of his difference. I felt for him. It is painful when you understand you are the odd one out. The behaviors and conversations he shared about it pulled at my heartstrings.

Silas's realization about being different was not just about the feelings he had about it: These moments of clarity about being disabled were occasionally associated with significant behavior challenges. Silas's favorite professional basketball team was the Chicago Bulls, and his favorite player was Michael Jordan. The Bulls were the best team in the NBA at the time and had won three championships. When Michael Jordan took a hiatus from the NBA in an attempt to play professional baseball, this took Silas's beloved Bulls from being the best team to being just one of several good teams.

One day during the playoffs, the Bulls were playing against the New York Knicks. Silas was watching the game with staff and housemates, and the Knicks were winning the game.

I was working with Harry that day, and we were going to go for a walk at the park.

Silas said to me as I was leaving, "You know, we'd win if we just had Michael Jordan. No one could beat the Bulls with Michael Jordan, Michael Jordan," as he rocked back and forth and paced the living room.

I replied, "You are probably right, Silas. They never beat the Bulls when Jordan was playing."

One of the female staff members became a little sarcastic and said, "I don't know, Silas. I think maybe the Knicks are just the better team."

Silas appeared to ignore her comments, and I didn't give the situation much thought. Harry and I went for our walk, but when we arrived back to the group home, there was a chair from the living room halfway across the front yard. I could hear Silas yelling, "If you keep messin' with me, I'm gonna fuckin' kill you!" When we got inside the house, Silas's assigned staff member was visibly terrified. I asked her to work with Harry, and I went up to the third floor to find Silas in his room.

He was irate. Silas relayed that when the Bulls lost, the staff member had said, "See, I told you so." It was a reckless and unprofessional comment. The staff member, unfortunately, did not consider the impact of using sarcasm with Silas.

Silas felt he was being mocked, so he took her sarcasm personally. He could not cope with his feelings about the sarcastic comment, and so he had picked up a fairly heavy chair, taken it through the front door, and heaved it from the front porch onto the yard.

It was an unfortunate situation, a reminder of the importance of choosing words carefully. All I could do was remind him of his talents and his goodness, and redirect him. Aside from destroying property and the temporary intense feelings of the moment, he was hurting. His lip quivered and he looked to me and said, "Why did I have to be born this way, man?"

CHAPTER 9

Heidi

Heidi represents those who needed support beyond the role we traditionally consider and whose behaviors appeared to be affected by less common stimuli and contexts. Other than occasionally spitting when distressed, Heidi's challenging behavior was self-directed: hitting her head with the base of her palm and biting her index finger. It took considerable effort by all those who supported her to begin piecing puzzles together to help her through the unusual things that she found upsetting and aversive. It truly does take a village to help a person grow, and I was just one small part of a larger group of people supporting her. Heidi helped me learn to operate within a team, and I am grateful to her for that.

• • •

"Your first name is Andrew. Your last name is Houvouras: H-o-u-v-o-u-r-a-s. You were born December 14."

Heidi was 16 years old, and the ability to recall these facts and express them in this manner was typical of the way she interacted with people, young or old. She would approach people and request this information when she met them, and she possessed the ability to accurately recall it if asked or if she encountered the person again.

With a huge vocabulary and an affinity for flowered dresses, the ability to read, and a love of drawing, Heidi also had unique abilities often described as savant or genius. Of course, autism is hardly homogenous. As it did with Heidi, it presents in each individual in a unique, idiosyncratic manner, leading to popular sayings among those in the field such as "If you have met one person with autism, you have met one person with autism." Heidi, like all the people I have met, was unique. She enjoyed brushing her long, light brown hair and expressed an interest in brushing and styling the hair of her female housemates and staff.

Sitting as a model for Heidi's drawings was one way of pairing with her, although she did not draw all the staff members at the center. She had her preferences about people, and these models tended to resemble her. She preferred to draw long-haired White females or the other children. Her pictures were always drawn in pencil with the person in a standing position. The person's full name and birthday were written across the top of the portrait. Heidi did seem to like me and remembered many facts about me, but I was not one of her preferred models (a humbling fact).

The boy band craze was all the rage while Heidi and her peers were living in the residential center. The young girls watched music videos; listened to CDs; and had numerous discussions that bordered on arguments about which boy was the most handsome, the best dancer, or the smoothest singer. Heidi largely presented as fairly stoic, but she and one of her roommates were adamant that Lance was the cutest and most important member of the band *NSYNC. It was a piece of normalcy in a small community that was not considered normal, and staff members were happy when our residents reveled in being young.

Heidi's penchant for remembering birthdays was a bit paradoxical, as her own birthday was a source of great consternation. As often happens in psychology and behavior analysis, we sometimes stumble into important findings. One day, we were throwing a birthday party for one of the children on the unit. As the children sat in the dining area, Heidi appeared visibly agitated. When the collective singing of "Happy Birthday to You" began, she brought her index finger to her mouth, clenched down with her teeth briefly, began shaking, and threw her cupcake across the room. She jumped up out of her chair, breathing heavily. While it was my first time seeing this, the staff let me know it was not the first time it had happened.

We asked Heidi to sit on the couch or go to her room. She scurried to her room, where she bounced lightly on her bed, talking quietly to herself, extending her arms out in front of her, and shaking her hands. I was the only behavior analyst there at the time, and Heidi was not my client. I asked one of her preferred staff members to come with me to talk with her. The staff member and I knocked on the door (which was open), entered, and the staff member asked, "What is it, Heidi?"

Exasperated, Heidi cried, "You will not turn 18! You will not get older! You will not grow up! You will not die!" Tears streamed down her face as she sobbed, repeating the phrases softly as the familiar staff member assured her things would be OK.

Both of us were shocked. Heidi was just a little over a year from turning 18. For her, a birthday was not a cause for celebration but a torturous reminder of her impending mortality. It appeared 18, the age of consent and adulthood, was "old" to her and the beginning of the countdown for what little time was left.

I felt for her: To have the ability to recall everyone's birthday came with a price. It was as much a curse as a blessing. Further discussions with her staff member also showed she could recall the dates of people's passing (mostly historical figures) and would mention this often. Here was a person with skills and abilities that were quite advanced, but the perseveration on dates and dying haunted her.

I do not propose that her special abilities caused her to throw her cupcake. A behavioral perspective is vastly different from a psychologically oriented perspective. A simple explanation is that a behaviorist does not assign thoughts and feelings as causes of behavior. It is a subtle but important distinction. This is not to say thoughts and feelings are not important; they are. We acknowledge thoughts and feelings, as we have our own. The term we use for them is *private events*. Some of Heidi's private events terrified her.

Over the next month or so, Heidi's gift of language and her rich descriptions conveyed she loved being a child. For her, adults were old, and old people die. If I could have given her one gift, it would have been perspective, but perspective is gained, not given.

Once we figured out the birthday issue, we found solutions. Choice matters. Heidi was always asked if she wanted to participate in others' birthday celebrations. More often than not, she chose to participate, and the birthdays came and passed without Heidi becoming upset.

A little more than a year later, Heidi turned 18. And she chose to have a birthday celebration, happy and untroubled about this milestone. What had changed to bring her to the point of acceptance? I still do not know. She had progressed and adapted.

Fears are strange. We ruminate on them. We avoid dealing with them, reinforcing our avoidance. We sometimes forget that at times we each may be one of the silent—and that silence is often only a matter of degree—as we go through our experience of life in all of its complexity, with no easy answers as to how to cope with whatever plagues us.

Just like Heidi, I too sometimes feel like throwing a cupcake as I consider my own mortality. Who doesn't? To feel the pain and confusion of the silent as we face those things and events in life that we do not understand is to be truly human. In this case, Heidi was fortunately able to weather this storm. Despite her expansive vocabulary, Heidi could not articulate how she got to this point of abandoning her fear nor explain how she thrived as she got older, leaving residential treatment eventually for a less restrictive setting. Whatever fears plagued her, I hope they are gone. I hope that somewhere, she is drawing pictures and making people feel special by recalling their birthdays.

CHAPTER 10

Joey

Of course there were challenges, but the bulk of the time I spent with the silent was fun. Joey was fun. We laughed. We learned. We lived life—walking, talking, listening to music, and visiting places he had never seen. There were small moments at meals, birthdays, and holidays. There was the repetition of teaching daily living skills. There was the awareness that some of these people, like Joey's housemates, had been locked away from the world and were now free to live in homes and nice communities. This was balanced by the realization that for some of the people described here, their needs demanded specialized service and support to be found only in tightly controlled, restrictive settings.

Problem behavior was a concern for many of the people introduced here. Joey's problem behavior, if we can call it that, was expressed in unique ways, some of which I have never experienced before or since. If the schedule said "Joey," you knew your shift was going to be interesting. Joey had the uncanny ability to always make you feel like you were helping him progress. One of these abilities was his talent for remembering and using staff names.

This was not always the case with my clients. In my experience, among the many people served by the agency, this was a rare skill. From the first day, detailed here, I enjoyed working with Joey, and as I hope you will learn, he enjoyed working with me.

• • •

One cold spring Friday, around midmorning, I received a phone call from our program director asking me if it was possible for me to come to the group home to help with a new resident. I agreed and headed over.

Joey, the son of a small-town librarian in West Virginia, was moving into the group home. As his mother had gotten older, she realized he needed more support than she could give. So, she reached out to the agency to find him an appropriate residence. I was told they knew little about Joey or about his behavior, so they wanted me to come to the group home to help assess his situation.

They had also called another staff person to provide additional support. The other staffer they called in was a real character—a colleague and friend named Aaron. He had been a former postal worker and would talk proudly about his time in that position; by his own admission, however, he was not the world's most patient person. Aaron was into cars, and while he was extremely kind to the residents, he was easily frustrated and exasperated by problem behavior. He lived relatively close to the group home, a coincidence that would have a significant bearing on Joey's story.

When Aaron and I arrived at the group home, Billy, the program director, was there with Joey. It was just before noon, and the other residents were out at their morning program. Billy introduced us to Joey and spent a few minutes telling us what little he knew, then left. In front of us, slowly pacing the group home floor, was a young man who appeared to be in his early 20s. He was 5-foot-8 and had fair skin and dark hair. When he walked, he kept his head tilted down with his eyes looking up. At first, he didn't say much as he walked at a slow pace, scanning everything with his eyes.

Then, in a high-pitched half scream, he started speaking in the third person: "Upset! Upset! Joey's upset!" Walking over to the television cabinet, he placed his hands on top of the television and engaged in a rocking motion. In these days, televisions were wide and clunky and were housed in thick, sturdy wooden cabinets situated low to the floor.

"Joey's going to break TV!" He persisted, using whatever strength he could muster. The TV refused to budge.

"Upset! Upset! Joey's upset!" he reiterated as he headed toward his room. Crisis averted … or so we thought as we followed him.

"Upset! Upset! Joey's upset!" he said as he walked from his room into the living room. His volume escalated as his frustration apparently mounted. "Joey's going to break the couch!"

The couch, like the TV, had a strong wooden base and was heavy. As we did not know Joey or his physical capabilities, Aaron and I realized maybe we had underestimated him, and we prepared for the worst—but the worst never came. Just as his attempts at the TV were thwarted, the size of the couch was more than a match for Joey's intentions.

While Joey's behavior never escalated into a physical assault, his verbal onslaught was just beginning. Sauntering up to within a foot of us in a deliberate, paced manner, he stared up from the top of his eyes with his head angled down and yelled, "Upset! Joey wants to ride in the car! Upset! Upset!"

I looked at him and said, "Joey, the van is with the other residents. It will be here in a little while—"

Interrupting me, he said, "Upset! Upset! Joey's upset. Joey wants to go in the van."

Using a tried-and-true therapeutic technique, I calmly repeated, "Joey, the van is—"

"Upset! Upset!" Joey yelled as he approached Aaron. "Joey's upset!"

Aaron looked nervous. Many of the clients Aaron and I worked with were inclined to be aggressive or self-injurious. Having been unsuccessful with his attempts at breaking the TV and couch, would he try to break Aaron or me? To our great relief, the answer was a resounding "No"—unless you can break someone by screaming, something he almost succeeded at with Aaron.

For what seemed like hours but was probably only 15 minutes, Joey repeatedly walked away, turned around, and came back, repeating the same refrain: "Upset, Joey's upset! Want to go in the van!"

Each redirect typically resulted in more yelling, often inches from our faces. It was loud, repetitious, and even became predictable. Joey stopped requesting the van and began screaming, "Upset! Upset! Joey wants books." The return of the screaming riled my coworker.

What we would learn in the coming weeks was that Joey's mother had taught him to read, and as she was a librarian, his life was filled with a love of books. At the time, we didn't know any of this. Facing my redirections, "We can go to the mall and the bookstore when everyone gets back," Joey began to exclusively go to Aaron: "Books! Upset, Joey wants books!" Aaron's level of agitation rose and rose with each statement. Finally, he broke.

"Listen, man, stop yellin'! We will go in the van. We will go to the mall and get some books. Heck, I'll get you *Playboy*, but stop yellin' at me!"

"Hey, Aaron, it's OK; I got this," I interjected as I stepped between them.

Joey suddenly said, "Joey wants to go to the mall!" and the yelling completely stopped.

For the next hour or two, everything was going well, with Joey emerging from his room, saying in a much lower volume, "Joey wants to go to the mall."

No broken TVs, no broken couches, and no screaming.

When the residents arrived back home, Aaron, Joey, and I took the van to the local mall. We entered through a major department store, planning to walk through it to a bookseller. As we made our way through the store, we came into the cosmetics department.

An elegant woman in a navy dress walked up to Aaron, Joey, and me and said, "Would you like to try this cologne for men?"

Joey looked up at her in his idiosyncratic manner, head down, eyes up, and yelled enthusiastically, "Joey wants *Playboy*!"

The woman looked at the three of us, eyes bulging, and walked away.

What we didn't know at the time was that Joey demonstrated delayed echolalia, the propensity to parrot back something that had been said minutes, hours, or even days earlier.

Lesson learned.

Aaron, Joey, and I walked to the bookstore and browsed around, and Joey picked out two books to bring to his new home.

The group home work happened in shifts. I typically worked my preferred shift, 7:00 a.m.–3:00 p.m., on weekends. One morning, I arrived at the group home a few minutes early and met with Larry, the overnight staff member, to debrief on how the overnight shift went. Larry looked exhausted, not all that unusual for those working the 11:00 p.m.–7:00 a.m. shift.

In his quiet way, Larry said, "Man, it's been a long night."

This was unusual, as the overnight shifts were rarely taxing except for being tiring, as the residents were almost always asleep around 10:00 p.m.

"What happened?" I asked.

"Oh, my gosh," said Larry. "We just got back from the hospital."

Just as Larry began his story, Aaron walked in, just shaking his head.

Larry proceeded to tell me the story: "Last night I went to the bathroom. When I went to do room checks, Joey was not in his bed. I noticed Robert's door was open, and when I went to check it out, I noticed Robert's window was also open." Robert's room was on the second floor and faced the street, with a small piece of roof looking down on the sidewalk. "Out there on the edge of the small roof section, Joey was standing in his underwear! I leaned out the window and said, 'Joe, come back in!' and he looked at me and said, 'Joey wants to fly.'"

As Larry desperately tried to convince Joey to come back inside, Aaron, who lived just down the street, was driving home and spotted Joey on the roof. He parked his car; ran across the small yard; and heard Joey say, "Joey wants to fly!"

Aaron said, "Just go back inside, Joey."

Larry said, "Joe, you gotta come back inside, buddy. Come on back," and started to go out on the roof to try to reach him. Both men said they were in an absolute panic when the unthinkable happened.

Joey jumped off the roof, falling directly onto the sidewalk.

Aaron rushed to his aid, and Larry hustled downstairs and out the front door. They were both worried about the extent of Joey's injuries. They called 911, and Larry accompanied Joey to the emergency room.

Behavior analysts tend to remain incredibly skeptical, but I think you could say it was a miracle that Joey only scuffed his

CHAPTER 10: JOEY

knees and hands. He did not break a single bone or chip a tooth or hit his head. He fell about 10 feet directly onto concrete and was merely scratched up and bruised. It could have been—and should have been—so much worse.

I cannot describe or overemphasize how fortunate he was. The two men telling me the tale had done everything they could to stop things from going awry. As they told the story, they shook their heads in amazement at Joey's luck. We then remembered having heard "Joey wants to fly" for a few weeks. It never occurred to us that this was what he meant.

Later that morning, Joey woke up while we were fixing breakfast. Aaron was Joey's assigned staff member that day.

When we all sat down for breakfast, Aaron looked over at Joey and said, "Joey, do you want to fly?"

Adamantly, Joey said, "No, no. Joey doesn't want to fly."

This whole scenario reminds me of how challenging life can be when there are deficits in communication. Joey knew what he meant when he said, "Joey wants to fly," but we had no clue. It reminds me how we often do not understand the complexities of human behavior. This entire event required some incredibly complex planning: Joey had to leave his room when his aide went to the bathroom, enter a housemate's room, crawl out through the window, and make the jump. All of this required some imagination and daring that none of us necessarily thought Joey had. It reminded me to not underestimate those I work with in any way.

Joey was generally a gentle, curious, and amiable person. His problem behaviors were minimal, but as we found out in the mall and on the roof, things sometimes happen that there is just no way to predict.

Joey was a sweet young man. I liked him from day one. I think he liked me. We can often come to realize what a profound impression and difference our clients make in how we live our lives. I think we hope that we have a positive impact on their lives. Years later, though, with some things left unsaid, it is an open question, and perhaps, even wishful thinking.

Several years after leaving the state, I returned for a relative's wedding. I was walking in a beautiful tree-lined park when I saw a group of people having a small cookout. I spotted Joey. I approached the young lady who was near him, introduced myself, and asked if it was OK for me to say "Hi" to him.

She turned to Joey and said, "Joey, there's someone here who wants to say 'Hi' to you."

I started to say, "Hey, Joey, it's been a long time—"

Before I could get another word out, he reached up, touched my face, tilted his head down, smiled, and said, "Andrew. Andrew. Andrew."

He remembered me.

SECTION 4
Navigating Transitions

Transitions are often discussed as a particular problem for those with autism and developmental disabilities. Transitioning has been the focus of substantial behavior-analytic research (Castillo et al., 2018; Jessel et al., 2016; Luczynski & Rodriguez, 2015). While much of the research literature addresses moving from a highly preferred activity to a less preferred activity or from one room to another, all of the people in this book faced even larger transitions, such as moving from a home to a residential treatment center or relocating from a specialized treatment center to a home (whether family home or group home). If the daily transition from one activity to the next can be difficult, how might we measure the difficulty of having to leave the only environment ever known as home; saying goodbye to the people providing care; and entering into a new location with new people, sights, sounds, and smells?

How do we begin to define a successful transition? A person moves to a facility where even access to a bathroom requires a key, all visible areas are covered by cameras, privacy is nonexistent, unfamiliar adult staff oversee all movement and activities, and roommates are randomly selected. If, by chance or design, their behavior improves, their families are absent, unable to share or celebrate the progress. Moving forward often means moving out. Shifting into the community from a facility would seem, at face value, more preferable. But is it? What if the facility is the only stable home that person has ever known? When, if ever, can a facility be an approximation of a home?

Hard questions must be asked and answered.

But the truth of the matter is that transitions are challenging for many people and may be compounded by a disability. Behavior analysts often look to enrich the environments of the clients as a means to prevent problem behavior. If you are transitioning a client, regardless of how small or big the transition, ask yourself, "What is in it for the person?" "What would mediate and make it easier for that person?" More often than not, the answer is increased *reinforcement*; increased availability of the things that person finds preferable. *Environmental enrichment* (providing an increased number of reinforcers freely available to someone) is not a permanent solution, but it is one way to try to make transitions a little less aversive and a little more reinforcing.

Although their stories are all different, I directly experienced the transitions into and out of various living arrangements for the five individuals in these chapters: Eddie, David, Jason, Jackson, and Mr. A. Number 1.

For those living in residential placements, group homes, and institutions, the first transition out of their home might very well be the last time they live at home with their family. If it sounds grueling, it should—because it is. Sometimes children end up thousands of miles away from their parents, as you will read in the stories of David and Mr. A Number 1. For some children, their only stable residence has been structured domiciliary care, as it was for Jason and Eddie. Some individuals leave their homes as children for what could amount to the rest of their lives, as was the case with Jackson.

Those of us working with the silent tend not to sit with this for very long. The more one thinks about it, the more disturbing it can become. So we go about our work trying desperately to serve others while not ruminating on the circumstances, the complexities, and the difficulties of transitions.

CHAPTER 11

Eddie

Those of us who have chosen helping professions or teaching often learn things we wish we did not know. Much of the time, they are small truths, things that make us chuckle or roll our eyes. When the big truths about neglect and abuse are learned, they hit hard and often produce a sinking feeling in the stomach and other visceral emotional reactions. Decades after meeting Eddie, I feel that same sensation when I think about him and his life circumstances. Even though Eddie was just a child when I met him, he had already endured great trauma in his life. How could I not feel that it was my job, at least in part, to protect him?

Eddie's story is triumphant, a testimony to his strength and how environments have the potential to cultivate skills, abilities, and evanescent periods of happiness. I have known many courageous people, certainly many of the people in this book are among them. But none showed the mettle of the young teenager I met shortly after beginning my first job as a certified behavior analyst. His story gave me pause that a dosage of empathy combined with behavioral science can fundamentally change a life.

• • •

Eddie was one of the toughest people I ever met. He was small and young and yet had unending confidence. I met Eddie shortly after he arrived on the center campus. He came to us wide-eyed, with short dark blonde hair, blue eyes, and a Southern drawl, in awe of his new surroundings. Considering where Eddie was from and what he had been through, his arrival on campus must have been an extraordinary deliverance. Born in one of the poorest parts of one of the poorest states in the country, he was the victim of horrific abuse at the hands of his parents. The campus of the center must have appeared to be a magical place. I felt the same way Eddie did when I first saw it, with its Spanish-tile-roofed concrete buildings, paved go-cart track, small animal pen, cafeteria for three square meals per day, pool, gymnasium, and fishing pond. Eddie probably never imagined a place like this existed before setting foot there.

As one of the first parts of a behavior assessment, professionals review client records. I almost wish I hadn't. The pages summarizing Eddie's history described the types of horrific abuse that make you question humanity. He was subject to things no person should have had to endure. Decades later, I still cry when I think about cigarette burns on his little arms, about his being starved and locked in rooms. Eddie's only crime was being born to people who never should have had children.

Removal from the birth home should have been an emancipation, the first step in the universe righting an egregious wrong and giving Eddie the gift of simply being a child. Our systems to protect children, though, are hardly foolproof, and the move to foster care was just a change of circumstances that may have been free from abuse but proved to lack the personnel, expertise, and stability Eddie needed to make progress toward a more normalized life.

Normal may be impossible to define, but I like to think it means, at the very minimum, waking up in the same place knowing in that place you have the reassurance of being fed and being free from aversives, and that it is a place where you will be understood. The first two criteria, most places can provide; the last one, not so much. All the therapy, commitment, and love cannot replace the benefits or the horrors of one's unique learning history. While rarely the sole determinant of behavioral concerns, our learning histories seem to follow us. As we gain experience, what we have already learned can help us progress and grow, or it can hinder our ability to relate to others or learn new things.

Foster care was, at best, ineffective for Eddie. He bounced from home to home. By the time he arrived on campus, just shy of his 13th birthday, since being liberated from the hell he never chose, he had been in 13 different foster care placements. One day, when a staff member who repeatedly questioned my programming suggested my behavior plan was not "tough enough" on Eddie, I sternly replied, "He has had cigarettes put out on his skin. There's no punishment we could use that would be worse than anything he has already been through." However harsh it came across, I think the point had to be made. To go through hell and survive it as he did can render the use of aversives ineffective, ethically questionable, and morally reprehensible. And it clinically presents a challenge as to how to help the person exist in a world that is sometimes unaware and/or indifferent to prior suffering.

To this day, Eddie is one of my few heroes. He was determined and resilient. One of the highest privileges on campus was being permitted to help one of the staff in the maintenance of the go-carts, and Eddie made it his mission to achieve this goal. His problem behaviors were many: aggression (though minimal), significant property destruction, making threats, directing profanity and racial epithets toward others, and leaving rooms or buildings without permission. As the smallest of the children in his age range (13–15), he was regularly teased and taunted by older, larger children. He never backed down and made it abundantly clear he was not the person to bother.

Eddie did have physical altercations with his peers. In a unit where several residents were there for treatment of aggressive behavior, there was a constant awareness of what we needed to do to reduce the probabilities of conflicts. One of the things we did with Eddie (and some of his same-age peers) was practice and richly reinforce "calming down." When I came to the unit, this was one of the first programs I developed. Around campus, there were large plastic, sand-filled chairs. They were heavy to prevent them from being thrown, moved, or broken. If a child was acting up, the staff would say, "Time-out" or "Sit away." The children would go to the chairs for some brief period of time before rejoining their group or activity. I thought the language was bizarre and the plan reactionary.

In the new program, we did "practice runs" where we would say, "Sit down and relax," at various times throughout the day. During these practices, Eddie would smile and say, "Why are we doing this?" When he sat down, we would thank him, offer him a choice of his favorite treat/snack, and engage him in conversation. With Eddie, the plan worked to perfection. I remember being called to the unit from my office one morning when Eddie was getting into a heated argument with another child who was more than a foot taller than him. The staff said, "Sit down and relax." Eddie walked toward the chair, all the while yelling, "I am going to kick your ass! ... Fuck this, I am not going to do this shit!"—but he sat down in the chair. I wish I could tell you all my programs were this effective. They were not. They never are. Eddie had been to hell and back. In designing his program, we needed to put components in that addressed the behavioral concern but also were sensitive to the things he had been through in his past by being proactive and gentle.

It took Eddie a few months to work through the unit system and his individualized behavior plan, but he ended up earning the opportunity to work on the go-carts. He would spend hours outside working under the small covered "garage" where the go-carts were stored. Once a go-cart was serviced, it had to be tested. The smile on Eddie's helmeted face as he sped around the track each time was a small moment of perfect bliss, those moments every child, but especially this one, deserved.

Eddie's circumstances made me appreciate small things and question much of what I thought about relationships with and the subjective reality of the silent. More of our times than not were good times. We laughed—a lot. We talked—a lot. Eddie was inquisitive and would ask questions about professional wrestling, sports, movies, and video games—and about those of us who worked with him. When you saw him, you had to be prepared for a verbal onslaught of questions and conversations. He talked quickly, loudly, and constantly. The family he lacked, he replaced with his fellow residents and staff. The unit became the home he never had. Most of us cannot grasp this reality: a home where every door was locked (including bathrooms), where the walls were undecorated, personal possessions few, and home-cooked meals replaced by the three squares in the cafeteria. To us, it might be cold and sterile. To Eddie, it was everything. On Halloween, children often dressed up as their heroes or as something they aspired to be. Eddie decided to dress up like the staff, a reminder of how massively the day-to-day actions and little acts of kindness matter in ways we do not imagine.

A clever boy, Eddie always surprised people with his insights, sometimes divulging gossip he had overheard from the staff, and at other times, asking questions about the other children from his observations. He was particularly kind and helpful to the younger children who did not speak, many of whom were also my clients. Although he appeared to find being kind to the younger children reinforcing, he did not always act similarly to the older children nor to some of the staff.

As Eddie progressed, the one behavior that stubbornly persisted was profanity directed at others. In his assigned classroom, there were two male children and one female staff member whom he did not like (the staff member would eventually be caught stealing from other staff: Eddie read people well). If they bothered him or directed him, he would offer them some choice words. When the teacher measured it, he averaged 30 occurrences of directed profanity every 30 minutes: one per minute. They were mostly a tapestry of profanities and insults, laced together in one or two tirades for maximum effect.

To counter the behavior, we developed a *differential reinforcement of low rates of behavior* (DRL) program where Eddie would earn a reinforcing activity of his choice if he met the criteria for slowly decreasing numbers of directed profanities. In just a few weeks, the behavior plan resulted in Eddie engaging in only three or so occurrences of the problem behavior every 30 minutes. We were succeeding wildly. What we didn't know was Eddie's ability to decipher his programs. As his therapist, I was often part of the chosen activity: Eddie choosing to fish with me in the pond, shoot baskets, or toss a football.

One afternoon, Eddie had spent the better part of 30 minutes in class, doing his work. I called the classroom, and his teacher reported he had a very good day and wanted me to take him fishing when he earned the privilege. Upon entering the classroom, I looked over to Eddie, who looked at the clock and then toward the despised staff member. "Aw, man, I haven't cussed at all in the last 30 minutes," he said as he stared at the staff member, smirked, and said, "Fuck you, fat bitch!" He stared at her, looked to his teacher, and said, "Well, that's only two of the three cusses I could say today. OK, it's time for me to go fishing with my therapist. Andrew, let's go."

The staff was bothered, but Eddie had met the criteria, so while I knew we would have to make some changes to the program, we spent the next 30 minutes outside of class fishing in the pond. We did modify the program so the behavior could not occur close in time to the reinforcing activity. I remember this day vividly not just because of Eddie's clever deduction and the way he used his behavior but because he landed a 2-foot-long gar, a fish resembling an alligator with a long snout and sharp teeth. He got so nervous when it hit his line that he immediately handed me his fishing rod. He eventually reeled the gar in himself and stood proud, chest out and smiling from ear to ear, a temporary moment of perfection in an imperfect world. We carefully released the hook and placed the fish back in the pond. This was in a day before cell phones, so the picture of this catch is captured only in our minds.

I got to know Eddie well throughout his time at the unit. He made quick progress, figured out many aspects of his behavior plan, and was always one of our more advanced clients: physically, verbally, and intellectually. He reduced most of his significant problem behaviors, made academic progress, and actively participated in all aspects of his treatment. Such rapid progress would often lead to discussion about being discharged and would then be met by some significant behavioral demonstration: Eddie would engage in a litany of problem behaviors, losing his level and privileges, and ending months of documented progress.

The first two or three times, the treatment team thought little about this, but it became glaringly apparent that Eddie was sabotaging his treatment as it would lead to him leaving the center. It made sense to all members of the team: Eddie's progress produced discussions of moving away from the center, something he did not want to happen. The center was the only normal place he had ever known; the thought of transitioning away to someplace unpredictable was a legitimate fear, a road Eddie had already walked too many times in his short life.

Systems do not always serve children well. For Eddie, for once, the system and universe aligned in his favor. The center was part of a large organization with treatment centers in several states. The behavior analyst who replaced me when I left worked within the organization so that Eddie would be accepted into one of the company's adult residential treatment centers in the Midwest when he turned 18. He would be able to have continuity in his life and the stability denied to him as a child. While I don't know what happened to this clever young man, his resilience remains with me. He had every reason to be bitter, angry, and disengaged but instead smiled easily, was curious, and enjoyed making friends. I hope he has found his home, and I hope that home fits him wholly.

CHAPTER 12

David

Professionals dedicated to serving the silent are often commended for their patience. We are told we are caring, tolerant, and tempered. I have even heard, "It takes a special person to do what you do." The repertoires required to serve the silent, though, are hardly innate. They are learned, forged through exposure, rehearsal, training, reinforcement, and punishment. Whatever temperament, words, and actions we emit are by-products of experience and environmental contingencies. With the silent, observation supersedes insight, so the difficult days, the quiet or the chaos, and the necessary repetitions are all part of the learning equation.

David, who could speak but more often than not was silent, was probably more patient with me than he should have been. As a newbie to applied behavior analysis (ABA), I was charged with supervising his case. With his penchant for the dramatic, his behaviors and the circumstances they occurred under were unusual, even in settings where unusual was part of the norm. David, in the time he had been at the center, had made only marginal progress. But then, we stopped hypothesizing so often and did three things instead: listened, observed, and tested. The cumulative result was a marked improvement for David—improvements that ultimately allowed him to move back close to his family.

• • •

In my first week on the job as a behavior analyst, I spoke with the center's group home manager and we agreed I would go to the group home that Saturday around lunchtime to meet several of the staff and have lunch with the children. The center had a group home in a neighborhood approximately 30 minutes away. In the home lived six children whose behavioral data indicated they had made progress living on the unit and were deemed by their support team to be ready for "stepping down" to a less restrictive setting. I was to be working as their behavior analyst. On a beautiful, sunny February Saturday, I arrived at the group home right as lunch was being served. Because I was new to the job and wanted to make a good impression, I dressed nicely: pressed navy slacks, black belt and shoes, and a plaid green-and-blue-collared shirt from the Gap.

Sitting on a shaded picnic table with his head down, seemingly avoiding eye contact, was David. At just 13 years old, he was approaching 5 feet, 10 inches tall. David had a large vocabulary but could go days without uttering a word. Talking seemed to be laborious for him. His voice was deep and gruff for one so young. He was one of several children in a delightful, loving family, and his primary behavior was tearing clothing—his and others. When David's parents flew across the country to the center with him, they had to wrap him in a sheet, as he had torn all of his clothing off. He tore clothing: his, yours, someone else's; destroying it. White, Black, brown, male or female, young or old, David did not discriminate. My first functional assessment would be centered on this behavior.

The group home staff brought me closer to the table as one of the staff members grilled hot dogs and hamburgers. We went around the table introducing ourselves to one another. It got to be David's turn for introduction just after he had been handed a hot dog. I made eye contact with him and said, "Nice to meet you, David. You want some ketchup?"

David looked at me, growled, "No ketchup!" put both hands on the lower collar area of my shirt, and tore it right down the middle.

I remember standing there as staff rushed in, but the incident ended as quickly as it began, and I said, "I guess you don't want ketchup." And, no, I didn't ask about mustard. I had been initiated. The torn shirt was the only hiccup in the day. The staff got me a T-shirt and we all sat down and had lunch, with David peering at me from the corner of his eyes before he moved on to shoot baskets at the basketball hoop.

After this incident, I had no idea why David had torn my shirt. Was it because I was unfamiliar? Did I get too close to him? Was ketchup not something he wanted that day? While I did not know, I did not say, "It happened for no reason." The emerging behavior scientist knew differently: There is always a purpose, a function, to behavior. During his time at the center, the treatment team had surmised he did not like the feel of certain clothing items, and they bought tagless T-shirts and underwear and removed the tag from pants. His clothes were also mostly cotton, as the team believed he was more sensitive to synthetics. By the time David and I had our dramatic introduction, he no longer tore his own clothing, only other people's. The answer to why this persisted evaded the behavior analysts and the medical professionals serving the center and the group home, who would wax philosophical about the possible reasons. It is not easy to identify behavior function. There are a myriad of reasons as to why a person engages in any behavior.

Within a few weeks, we were hard at work doing David's evaluation to learn more about his tearing behavior. Tearing was not new to David. It was one of the major reasons he was at the center. We were going to do a particular assessment called a functional analysis. As I had never run a functional analysis, two of my mentors would be sitting in and coaching me, but they primarily served as observers. It just so happened that the state agency overseeing the center and group home were conducting a surprise audit, and four of the most renowned professionals in the field of behavior analysis were in town and would be observing part of the evaluation. Talk about pressure!

I sat at a table with David. He was dressed in a T-shirt and jean shorts. I wore tan slacks, a white shirt, and a Jerry Garcia tie. The first session was called an "ignore" condition, where the tearing would be ignored. David would attempt to stare at me, getting within about a foot of my face. If he reached for my tie or for my button, I was to say nothing back to him and block further attempts. If he popped a button, I was to remain placid and poker-faced. The evaluation went fine, with David engaging in few incidents of tearing regardless of how we arranged the environment. He did pop off two of my buttons, and my tie, while not yanking or choking me, had to be cut off due to how tight David had pulled it. Unfortunately, amid the many mistakes I made and the peculiar nature of problem behavior, we did not uncover the reason behind clothes tearing in this session.

The answer, however, would soon come.

During the day of my initiation, I noticed several of the staff wore tattered-looking shirts over their uniform shirts. With no definitive results from the evaluation, I decided to talk less and listen more. On my next visit to the group home, at a loss for answers, I asked one of the staff, "Why do you guys all wear those torn shirts?" The direct-care staff said, "You guys are running all these fancy evaluations and have all those staff and support at the center. We don't have that here," as the group home was about 20 miles away from campus.

"We figured out a long time ago: David tears clothing if you make eye contact. We wear these shirts and tape them so if David puts his hand on a shirt, we can look away. If we look away, David will not tear. And, if he does tear, he's only undoing the tape from the old shirt."

For the next few hours, the residents, staff, and I had lunch, played board games, and then went outside to the spacious yard that included the basketball hoop. The same staff member who had told me about eye contact being the *function*, the "it" factor to the behavior, was rebounding a basketball for one of David's housemates. David approached her and put his right hand on her shirt and pulled at it. Doing just what she had told me, she looked away and began talking to the housemate. David moved his head toward the staff's head. She calmly turned her head away. David put two hands on her shirt.

The calmness and bravery of the staff member cannot be overstated. She was interacting with a person with a long history of tearing clothing, which could leave female staff exposed. Unafraid, undaunted, she was the consummate professional, disciplined, and composed. After about 15 seconds, David dropped to the ground dramatically, yelled, and remained at her feet for about a minute before getting up and meandering around the yard again.

In our evaluation, set up by some of the brightest behaviorists in the field, we had tested the incorrect variable. We were too busy listening to one another instead of the people in the trenches, doing the daily work and constantly observing David and his behavior. Armed with this revelation, we arranged a test where if he touched my shirt, I would look at him. The result? Torn every time. The other condition involved looking away when he touched the shirt, which resulted in him walking away ... every time.

It is fair to ask, "Was it difficult to get the staff at the center's school to look away?" The answer was, "Yes." It took significant convincing to get the staff to implement the "looking away" program because their histories were filled with having their shirts torn. With the new behavior plan in place and implemented with fidelity, David's tearing began to decrease. After a constant reduction for 3 months, tearing no longer occurred until David was discharged—except for one final time.

Over the course of the year, David continued to grow. His physical maturation was accompanied by fewer problem behaviors and, thanks to his speech-language pathologist and the direct-care staff, a marked increase in speaking. David was never conversational, but he did learn to ask for his preferred foods, drinks, and activities. As his tearing was now nonexistent, he moved closer to being discharged and returning to his hometown on the other side of the country.

With few behavior challenges, there were few restrictions on what David could do, so a class outing to SeaWorld® was a nice break to his typical schedule. A month or so prior to this trip, I had accompanied David to Walt Disney World® with his family. It was a wonderful time watching a family be a family, and it went off without incident.

This day had gone similarly; the travel to the park and the day were stress-free ... until we were leaving the polar bear exhibit with a large crowd. The other residents and staff were about 20 feet in front of David and me. David was walking slowly and appeared distracted. All of a sudden, I noticed his hand on his face, and when he pulled it away, he was bleeding from the nose. David looked visibly shaken. I said calmly, "Let's go find you a tissue." He looked at the blood on his hand and belted back, "No tissue!" grabbed my shirt, tore it but held on to it, and dropped to the floor. I dropped with him to the ground as he held on tightly while lying in a fetal position.

Out of the shadows came the security guards. "Stop fighting!" they commanded.

• • •

This was not my first rodeo. A few years prior, a flu was spreading throughout the agency and I filled in at one of the group homes for a client named Rudy. One of his favorite activities was going for a car ride. So on a cold and rainy day with the ground dusted with late-season snow, Rudy and I went on a car ride. After perhaps 30 minutes, we were returning home. To get to the driveway, we had to drive over a small bridge that was 10–15 feet above a creek. We were going very slowly due to the mud, slush, and snow when I looked over at my passenger seat where Rudy was sitting. He looked at me, reached down to undo his seatbelt, and began attempting to open the door. I threw my car in park and must have moved at superspeed to get to the other side, where Rudy was attempting to put his legs over the metal guardrail in what was assuredly going to be an attempt to jump into the shallow, rocky water below. I have no doubt he would have done severe harm had he succeeded. He was wearing a winter coat; I grabbed it as forcefully as I could and pulled him back. A very upset Rudy grabbed me back. He was strong and low to the ground, and we wrestled our way off the bridge, then tripped over one another, tumbling away from the bridge toward the little hill climbing to the house.

While few people were outside on this cold, dreary day, local law enforcement were on the job, and two of them just so happened to see these two grown men "fighting." Kudos to them, they did not draw their guns but did pull up, lights on, and say, "You two, stop it! What's going on here?" Muddy, wet, and tired, I just looked at them and said, "Guys he's autistic and lives here at this house. He can't talk. Can you help me get him up to the house?" The officers graciously lent a hand. What was a dangerous situation in many regards ended up OK.

• • •

I hoped for a similar end to this crisis.

With David curled on the ground, his hands tightly gripped on my shirt, blood everywhere, my chest exposed, I looked at the guard closest to me, pointed to our lead teacher and the rest of our group about 75 feet away, and said, "Sir, we're not fighting. He's autistic and has a nosebleed. He's scared. Can you please hustle and grab the tall lady?"

The security team immediately went from defensive mode to great helpers. "What can we do to help?" they asked.

"Can you get us a ride out to the parking lot? I think our day is done," I said.

David's fear was abating as his nosebleed lessened and the moments passed. The security team called for a golf cart and went from being assertive to kind and supportive as the day at the park ended for David and his peers.

A few months after the incident at SeaWorld, David was being discharged. His parents flew into town, and David and I joined them to fly out west to his hometown, where he would be moving into a group home close to his family. The home, whose residents were all young men with autism, was spacious, clean, and homey. I attended the first day of high school with David, who was shown his schedule by a teaching assistant. David seemed nervous and happy.

Two days later, I returned to spend half a day with him as part of our transition plan. To everyone's surprise, David had learned his schedule, and without staff assistance, walked to his different classes without staff prompting! It was a level of independence no one would have anticipated in such a short period of time, a healthy reminder for us to think and focus less on disabilities and more on abilities.

The things that shape our actions within helping professions and behavioral science are sometimes born of calamities and successfully resolving them. Almost 30 years later, I might not be so eager to take Rudy (or any other client) in my car or David to SeaWorld. But I like to think I would. I would like to think we are more aware, and it is not necessary to have Autistic Day at the Park; it's just OK to have autism and be at the park.

The predicaments with David (and Rudy) helped lay the foundation for similar types of events in my development as a professional and my ability to remain calm amid trying circumstances. It was a shaping process unintentionally implemented by the most effective of my instructors, the silent.

CHAPTER 13

Jason

We are all prisoners of reinforcement. Whether we are cognizant or unaware, reinforcement establishes, shapes, and modifies our behavior. As clinicians, when we become fluent in different assessments, reinforcement has great benefits—we more quickly respond affirmatively to appropriate behavior and become more diligent about collecting accurate data. The reality of reinforcement also means we will engage in similar actions under similar stimulus conditions. We may go back to engaging in an action and making a decision that previously produced the desired behavior change. We may be less inclined to individualize a new set of procedures and, instead, retreat to the therapy or procedures with which we had past success.

I was drawn to ABA, in part, due to its emphasis on individualized assessments and behavior plans. To me, it was and is logical, systematic, and humane. Working with Jason hammered home the importance of analyzing the contingencies of therapeutic actions.

Do we assign children to groups and therapies based on belief systems and what we have done before, or do we take into consideration client preferences? In this regard, Jason was my greatest teacher and reminded me to remember that whatever someone is recommending therapeutically requires an evidence base AND a frank discussion with the client and their assent.

We all live and learn, but we could have spared Jason unnecessary agony and upset if we had been wise enough to avoid assuming a certain therapy would be an effective treatment modality. The silent deserve to have us asking questions about risks versus benefits. Just because what we do is called "therapy" does not mean it is necessarily therapeutic, nor does it mean that it produces a desired outcome.

• • •

With his short-cropped dark blonde hair and thick eyebrows, Jason favored khakis, sportscoats, bow ties, and thick-rimmed glasses, and he often carried a briefcase. He often dressed the part of an adult, even as a young man. He looked like a young professor, a look he cherished as the most intellectually advanced of the residents on our unit at the center. Jason was a full reader, and in comparison with his peers, had advanced academic skills. He relished his role as a sophisticate.

On a cold October day, after only 5 days for both of us in a new city and state, I stopped by Jason's group home in the Northeast, a home that would be his home for perhaps the remainder of his life. I was telling him goodbye for the last time. We shook hands and parted ways. I never heard from him or about him again.

Adulthood, often determined somewhere between a client's 18th and 22nd birthdays, thrusts them abruptly from child to adult services. It was almost expected that Jason, at 18, was ready to live on his own because he was now legally an adult—albeit an adult who had never lived on his own, an adult without family or a support network. Our agency understood the arbitrary determination of adulthood and knew that transitioning out of the center was going to be a difficult proposition. Amy, one of my mentors, had established a program at our center based on a train-the-trainer model. For several years, clients who left our center often returned within a year, the receiving environments being ill-equipped to support their intensive needs.

In order to help clients who had just reached adulthood transition into new living environments, whether they were moving back to their family home, or into a group home as Jason was about to do, we began having a caretaker accompany the client and remain available for 2 or 3 days. Those few days could present some real challenges. The first day consisted of having the new caregivers perform a comprehensive review of records and, most importantly, becoming fluent in the proposed *behavior plan*, the "how to" document detailing the exact procedures that work for that person. The second day would involve daylong observation of the plan being implemented, and the third day would involve the guest running the plan under the supervision of the staff. It was a focused, effective model, quickly establishing the guest as an expert.

When the client would transition to a group home, the behavior analyst and often a client's preferred staff member would accompany them to their new home. Our program ran a fading plan, where one of us would spend the first night at the child's new home in case they needed to see a familiar face, with the other staff member being there for the day shift for about 8 hours the next day. Each day, we would gradually fade out the number of hours and the interactions we had with the client, coaching the parents and staff through the procedures and processes. On the last day, we would say goodbye, an often-emotional moment for the staff but not so much for the clients.

The plans were detailed, structured, and based on solid principles. This system dramatically reduced the recidivism rate. I was really grateful to Amy for her mentorship and handing me this program when she advanced within the company. It allowed me rare opportunities to go to different cities and states that I had never been to in my life, and to see the clients I had spent so much time with begin to spread their wings.

During his first night at his new home, I stayed the night. Jason came up to me and said, "Andrew, can I go to the bathroom?"

Being thrust into a life of independence was a challenge when you came from a center where every room, including the bathroom, was under lock and key. For 3 years, Jason had to ask permission from staff to unlock the bathroom door every time he had to go, an indignity in a world where safety and caution supersede all other considerations.

I said, "Jason you're in your home now and you never have to ask permission to go to the bathroom ever again."

For the next few days, I made it a habit of asking him to show me around the house or to find a particular item. I made a point to knock on his bedroom door and ask his permission to enter. Jason needed to recognize this home was his and the security and permission structure of a locked unit was, hopefully, forever a part of his past. Seeing him start to realize his increased freedoms, coupled with his astonishment at the realization of moving from limited to considerable choices, was affirming. Jason was on the path to a freer existence. He would need teaching, reinforcement, and support, but he was on his way.

Among my many clients, Jason's path to independence was an arduous one. Like many clients at the center, Jason was a ward of the state with no involved family, at least none we ever met. Jason was a ward of the state because of the horrific physical and sexual abuse he had suffered at the hands of his parents. Their rights had been deservedly terminated. This left Jason (and other children) with no one other than perhaps a guardian ad litem advocating for what was in their best interests. That person might periodically attend a monthly support meeting—but there was no confidant, no role model, no one to reminisce about important moments of days gone by, no one around to throw a birthday party.

Filling this role at our center were the behavior analysts. At this time, behavior analysts were certified by some individual states, and there were probably no more than several hundred certified in the largest states. Even in the early days of the profession, we were aware of the possible problems of serving in multiple roles; for example, the role of birthday party host was typically reserved for parents. On our unit, we took on this parental duty. I cannot imagine *not* serving in this role, particularly for children in a culture where birthdays are causes for celebrations. Throwing birthday parties, being a trusted ear, and advocating for the children were among the many roles we served even as we focused on analyzing behavior.

Prior to moving south with no other family, Jason began a shifting, unsuccessful journey through foster care, where the good intentions of many were overcome by the frequency and intensity of problem behaviors he would experience. Among the residents at the center who had suffered the indignities of abuse, this was a fairly normal path. If a relative was unable to step in to become a guardian, children's services stepped in. While they tried admirably, the marked lack of training, overwhelmingly ineffective bureaucracy, and reliance on sincere concern without evidence-based intervention was a recipe for failure.

Jason engaged in several significant problem behaviors. Two of the most challenging were physical aggression and fecal smearing. These behaviors clearly required a formal intervention. But in the late 1990s, behavior analytic services were still quite rare, especially in Jason's area of the country. Jason also engaged in some sexual activity with his peers who were also under the age of consent. This was a very serious concern. While this behavior did not appear to involve coercion or force of any kind on the part of either party to the interaction, this and Jason's other problem behaviors were of sufficient concern that the administrators in his home state sought more intensive services elsewhere. This brought him to our state and facility, hundreds of miles from his home.

Even Jason's initial placement at the center was complicated. Because he could speak, had an IQ higher than most of the children on our unit, and had some inaccurate diagnoses, it was presumed he would benefit from more traditional talk-based therapies, and he was placed on a different unit. It was a *topographical* approach, one where the form of his behaviors dictated the treatment. However, from a behavior analysis perspective, when what a behavior *looks like* (its topography) determines the treatment rather than the *function* of the behavior, the results of treatment tend to be hit or miss, and in Jason's case, it was a big miss. He needed his treatment to be based on function and on his unique individual characteristics. It was a problem for Jason and an ongoing problem in mental health approaches: Assumptions are made that a person can derive benefit from talk-based therapies before data suggest that is the case. He had the gift of speech, so it was incorrectly assumed that this gift could be turned inward, producing insight or reason that would provide rationales as to why he would do unusual things.

Jason's first unit was an abysmal failure. Thrown into a milieu with much more socially savvy children, several of whom had criminal histories, he was often teased or sexually propositioned. His reaction was to engage in a litany of problem behaviors. Specifically, he would smear feces on himself and laugh, scowl, and attempt to touch the other children with his filthy hands. Daily counseling sessions, weekly psychosexual group sessions, and a level system (wherein a progressive point-loss and earn-back system determines what privileges are available to the client at any one time) all proved completely ineffective. The professionals at the center wisely changed Jason's unit, which led to an immediate decrease in the frequency of his behavioral episodes.

One of the therapies at the center was the psychosexual survivors group. The children who had been sexually abused were often placed in groups broken up by gender and intellectual ability. Jason's group was supposedly tailored toward children with special needs. If you were sexually abused and had some type of developmental disability, you would attend the Tuesday afternoon groups. Children with average intellectual functioning or higher would attend the Wednesday morning groups.

Therapy, in this setting, was often based on the idea of how individuals process what is going on within the group. Group therapy really is not designed for a person who may think more concretely or even a person who has more well-developed verbal abilities but may not want to ruminate and revisit the traumas that they incurred when they were children, when they were helpless.

Jason was a young man keenly aware that he was different and mindful of the horrors he had endured. As he actively attempted to move on with his life, he was asked on a weekly basis to hear about abuse, revisit his own traumas, and talk with his peers about disgusting events. It was torturous, unfair, and not therapeutic for him.

One of the most important principles in ABA is the idea that client preference should guide the selection of reinforcers, goals, and objectives. Jason may have been my greatest teacher in teaching me the importance of preference. Jason was assigned to me when two of the other behavior analysts on the unit were having minimal success in helping him make progress.

Through careful observation and data collection, we found out that most of the behavioral episodes happened on Tuesdays in the afternoon or evening. With his aggressive and fecal-smearing behaviors increasing, I reviewed his previous assessments and behavior plans, but I was at a loss as to what the function of the behavior was. I decided to approach Jason and ask him if he could give me any insight into why he was having such significant difficulties on certain days and certain times. With tears in his eyes he said, "Andrew, I hate group and don't want to go anymore!"

For some of the children, I'm sure it was incredibly helpful to understand that other people have been through similar things and to be given professional assistance on different ways to talk and think about it. Jason, however, said, "I've been through some really horrible things in my life and get tired of having to be reminded about all the horrible things that happened to me every fucking week!" That was the last time Jason ever went to psychosexual group therapy.

Jason made incredible progress after leaving the group. In his remaining months on the unit, he may have had two more behavioral episodes, whereas before leaving the group, the episodes occurred weekly to multiple times per week. With the dissipation of these behavioral problems, we were able to focus on Jason's path to becoming an adult in the system's eyes and preparing him for his eventual discharge and the flight back north, where he would begin the next chapter of his life.

Jason spoke, and most importantly, we listened. I am too skeptical to believe removing him from the group was the key to his progress and discharge. I do think it brought him some comfort. I hope he has found some of the peace and happiness he was denied as a child.

CHAPTER 14

Jackson

It is often said the "journey of a thousand miles starts with a single step." Adopting a behavioral lens allowed me to appreciate the fact that a single step produces forward momentum and that many people's journeys are measured in the number of steps and not in miles. Jackson was just a boy when I met him, youthful, and smiling and laughing at many of the day's normal events. Some of the basic skills others master quickly took more time for him. But it wasn't just the amount of time needed. We also needed to break down tasks into their smaller parts, deliver affirmation and other reinforcers, and look closely at the data to help move Jackson closer to mastering single skills. This sometimes happened in a matter of days, but more often, it took weeks and months. Whatever time it took, though, reinforced an idea that was tested and testified to for decades by behaviorally oriented professionals: *Anyone* can learn—to be alive is to be capable.

Jackson made me appreciate small gains produced by small steps. We do not have to climb and conquer a mountain every day for our journeys to be filled with effort and accomplishment. We can spend so much time thinking about how to scale mountains that we no longer focus on what is right before our eyes. Jackson made me slow down and observe, to be in a moment and to watch for forward movement—which is often right before our eyes.

• • •

In the second week on my first purely behavior-analytic job, where I was doing direct clinical work and pursuing certification, I was asked to attend an intake meeting, a meeting that, unknown to me at the time, would have a lasting impact on me. At the center, a large multi-acre campus where children with severe challenging behavior lived and attended school, intake meetings were where parents or guardians met with the facility administrators and therapists to discuss, in great detail, items such as the location of their child's room, the on-site school, recreational facilities, the cafeteria, rules, services, and routines. The parents or guardians would sign a host of papers and finish by accompanying the child to their designated unit, leaving them for an indefinite period.

Walking into the conference room, I noticed there were three people at the table: a mother, a father, and a young lady in her late teens or early 20s. The mother and young lady, soon identified as the older sister, cried and held hands. On the floor underneath the table near the father and playing with toys sat the fourth member of the family—a beautiful little 7-year-old boy, long and thin with a big, white, tooth-filled smile and dark skin. As the meeting went on, he would periodically stand and crawl into his father's lap, make eye contact with him, smile widely, and kiss him before resuming his activities.

During the length of the meeting, even while interacting with his father, Jackson did not speak. His parents described him as nonverbal. Jackson was diagnosed with autism and profound

CHAPTER 14: JACKSON

intellectual impairment. I found it surprising that he was diagnosed as profoundly impaired because his parents spoke both English and Haitian Creole. Jackson could, in fact, do something I could not do: follow directions in either language. The youngest of three children, he was described by his family as loving and sweet. He walked with a smooth, graceful glide. He liked the water, though he did not know how to swim, and enjoyed swinging, spinning, and music.

His parents began to painfully describe the reasons why they were bringing Jackson to the residential treatment center. Jackson had been unable to stay in school as he was aggressive, often scratching, punching, and biting others. Sadly, these aggressive behaviors extended to himself as well; he would hit himself in the head or bite himself when he became frustrated. The most concerning self-injurious action, though, was head banging. Jackson would cock his head to one side and then violently shift his weight down on the corner of tables, doors, or chairs—ultimately resulting in numerous contusions and abrasions and, at times, stitches.

In addition to these severe behaviors, Jackson did not sleep well, so his father stayed up to watch over him at night to keep him safe. As a result, the father started falling asleep at his job and was ultimately unable to work. Out of despair and desperation, the family made the decision to bring Jackson to the residential treatment center and seek help there.

The move to a residential treatment center can be terrifying for a child and their family. Walls lack decorations, beds are nondescript, the paint is an institutional green, and privacy is limited as there are almost always roommates, and adult staff members are always present. Even bathrooms, like all other rooms and areas, are accessed only by unlocking doors. If a home is warm and inviting, then a residential treatment center is on the opposite end of the spectrum: cold and sterile.

Jackson's intake was incredibly sad due to his minimal communication skills and the intensity of his behaviors. The family was distraught at having to make this decision and leaving the baby of the family hundreds of miles from home in the care of strangers. My heart ached as Jackson reminded me of some of the clients I had worked with in adult residential treatment settings. I sat in that meeting with the stark realization this would be the first day of the rest of Jackson's life, where he would live in a facility, unlikely to ever return home.

I cannot fathom how a parent comes to terms with the fact that their 7-year-old child would be in someone else's care from that day forward; that they, despite their love and monumental efforts, were not equipped to handle the sheer amount of energy, hours, finances, and expertise necessary to make their son's life manageable, much less fulfilling.

The unit, or some other place like it, would be Jackson's home from that point forward. But it didn't look like a home. It didn't feel like a home. The reality of the meeting weighed heavy because Jackson needed so much—and while the center could provide much to help him, such places also involve an absolute loss of freedoms and choices, an absolute concession of control. Places like the unit, while sometimes necessary, are never ideal.

I remember the first weekend after the parents had left Jackson at the center and returned to their home. That weekend, Jackson's father came alone to visit his youngest son several hours from his work and other family members. This dedication to his son was very touching. When he arrived at the unit, Jackson approached him, but he did not hug his father nor did he smile. This was in stark contrast to his behavior toward his father during the intake and afterward, when they moved him into his room and the unit.

Jackson stayed within an arm's length of his dad for the entire visit, but he was not affectionate. They sat and ate lunch and walked around the playground together. Jackson sat on a swing as his father pushed him, but there was no joy.

After saying goodbye to his son, the father came into my office. Distraught, he began crying and said, "My son has forgotten me! It's only been a week, but he forgot who I was."

I hoped I could find the right words to comfort him.

"He hasn't forgotten you," I said. "He is probably mad at you. He may not understand exactly why you're not here every day, and he's adjusting to a new place. He doesn't appear to be scared, but I'm sure he's afraid. He is learning new routines, going to a new school, and he probably misses you. He may be mad at you, but he hasn't forgotten you."

Still crying, still distraught, he said, "I hope you are right, but I believe he has forgotten me."

He left shortly thereafter, and I did not know how things would resolve, as I was still new to children's residential treatment myself. I hoped the next visit would be different. I hoped there would be another visit.

The following week, the family called and said they would all visit on Saturday: the mother, father, brother, and sister. At that time, the behavior analyst at the center coordinated family visits, so as the behavior analyst, I planned to be at the unit on Saturday. I arrived at work early that morning, and things were fairly uneventful. Nevertheless, I was anxious about how the visit would go.

Security let me know when the family arrived. Every door, of course, was locked. I sat on a couch with Jackson about 30 feet from the entrance. A staff member had gone out to greet them and let them onto the unit. I heard the door opening as the family walked through the door. Jackson looked up and saw his family. He leaped up, ran across the room smiling, and jumped into his father's loving embrace. As they hugged, his father smiled, tears running down his face as he softly wept.

At the center, Jackson had some very typical and obvious preferred activities. He enjoyed music. When music was on, he would not dance but would instead rock back and forth rhythmically. He enjoyed playing with toys, especially toy cars and LEGO® bricks. As is sometimes the case with individuals with disabilities, the challenges would show up in idiosyncratic details. If Jackson was playing and putting LEGO bricks together, he would want to have every single brick immediately next to him, whether he was actively playing with it or not. A peer coming over to pick up a few pieces could produce crying combined with aggressive behavior to the peer, and sometimes self-injury. Staff had to be constantly vigilant, even when everything appeared uneventful.

Transitioning from one activity to another or from one location to another was difficult for Jackson. When I discovered he liked LEGO bricks, I thought a relatively simple procedure of *differential reinforcement of incompatible behavior* (DRI) would surely work. A DRI is when you directly teach and reinforce an action that cannot occur concurrently with the problem behavior.

In this case, because Jackson often made fists to hit others or himself, having him carry a small bag of LEGO bricks to the next environment occupied his hands in a different position and provided him with a known reinforcer. But given his need to have *all* the bricks, the small bag of bricks became a big bag, and the big bag became a small tub. Eventually, he was carrying a massive plastic tub of LEGO bricks around. This was never the intent of the DRI procedure, and I was responsible for allowing it. When I look back at how that procedure was ineffective, I realize I made a mistake. I was just so desperate for Jackson to stop hurting himself or other people.

CHAPTER 14: JACKSON

One of the skills Jackson mastered during my time with him was coloring, a skill taught and reinforced by his teacher, Rayna. At the time, other colleagues and professionals openly questioned the utility of whether Jackson should learn a skill such as coloring. However, the argument Rayna made was that by learning coloring, Jackson might be able to adapt to other parts of his community. A good example was going to sit-down restaurants, something rarely done by the clients at the center. It's not unusual for children and adults with disabilities to be relegated to eating fast food: The foods are fatty and tasty, the menus are limited, but the wait time is short.

Due to the difficulties clients sometimes experienced in the community, time away from the center was often limited, confining visits to the unit; hardly the warmest, most hospitable place for parents to spend time with their child. Options were then limited. A skill as simple as coloring served an important purpose. By learning to color, Jackson would be able to sit at a sit-down restaurant and engage in an appropriate activity while waiting for his food. Without that small behavior, Jackson would be forced to sit and wait while engaging in very few activities, since his leisure and play repertoire with respect to restaurants was not well developed. As he learned to color, he was also learning to wait and, ultimately, learning to tolerate visits at more family-friendly locales. Rayna's brilliant, well-executed idea made community outings more possible and enjoyable for Jackson.

Communication deficits are, of course, part of the diagnostic criteria for autism spectrum disorder and other types of disabilities. Communication was a challenge for Jackson. It was effortful and took time, quite often too much time. Jackson made very few attempts to echo sounds or words said by other people. When people have the ability to echo or parrot what is said (referred to in ABA terminology as an *echoic* skill or repertoire), it is easier to help them shape communicative responses. The absence of a reliable, echoic repertoire made it exceptionally difficult for Jackson to learn how to communicate. When echoing and picture exchange did not appear to be working well for him, his speech-language pathologist and assistant began teaching Jackson versions of American Sign Language (ASL). Jackson took to sign language more quickly than he did to attempts to echo back to staff or to select pictures.

Jackson was particularly fond of Skittles®. We were quickly able to teach him the sign for candy. By placing his index finger to his cheek and making a twisting motion, he could obtain candy. Of course, on Jackson's initial attempts, his index finger was placed toward the top of the crown of his head. This guided us to use a process called *shaping*, where we continued to reinforce approximations as we gently modeled and guided the twisting the index finger from the upper head to in and around the lower part of the cheek.

During Jackson's time in residential treatment, he only acquired about seven or eight *mands*, a behavioral term for a specific request. I cannot thank his team members enough, as it is difficult to capture how much work went into teaching him the seven or eight ASL signs that could help him acquire the reinforcers he wanted.

While seven or eight signs may not seem like much, to Jackson, the ability to ask for candy, or for a drink, or to play outside were considerable accomplishments, all actions that would end up making his life much easier.

Jackson was sweet, laughed easily, and formed tight bonds with several of the staff. He could be the most affectionate person, gently touching the faces of the people he liked. On our campus, there were small animals, and he would be very cautious and gentle when he was around them.

If you were only given this limited view of Jackson, you would question the appropriateness of his placement. Like all people, there were many facets to him. While he could be very affectionate, he could be incredibly violent to himself and others.

Headbanging may have been the most disturbing, dramatic, and dangerous form of self-injury, but his other forms were also upsetting to watch. Jackson would take his hand or arm to his mouth, clench down on the skin with his teeth, pull his mouth up, and stop only if and when he had done tissue damage. Less common forms of self-injury included pinching himself, biting parts of his body, and raising two fists above his head before striking down on his thighs. The results were bruises and cuts. As a result, Jackson often looked like he had recently been in a fight.

His aggression toward others was no less disturbing. Much like his self-injury, Jackson would headbang on others, once breaking a large staff member's collarbone. He would slam his fists onto another person's upper body and bite others—inflicting large pressure bruises that stung for days. In my decades working with individuals who demonstrate aggressive behavior, he is the only person to have ever bitten me. He bit me on my leg when we were attempting to physically restrain him for his own safety.

Restraint; prescription of psychiatric medications; and having an individual assistant, often referred to as a *one-on-one*, were just some of the efforts utilized to address Jackson's intensive problem behaviors and individual needs. The family had been unable to provide all that was required and made the painful decision to place him in residential treatment knowing it was the best decision for him. I look back on those days and know what we were trying to accomplish: We were trying to, first and foremost, keep him safe. Our focus was to design procedures as a way to decrease the occurrences of aggressive behavior to self and others and minimize the likelihood of injury.

I look back on that time when I was new to the field, and I question how effective we were. We took detailed data, graphed it, met regularly with a multidisciplinary team, changed things based upon the data, and wrestled with what methods to employ. I question the restraining, knowing fully well how necessary it was. I ask myself a multitude of questions: Would I do it today? Were the medications therapeutic? Did I monitor the case closely enough?

Jackson was well-staffed and well-supervised. Most of the staff, supervisors, and associated professionals followed protocol, and there were appropriate safety mechanisms in place. Now that I am well into my career, I ponder the complexity of his case as the ultimate example of relationships and intentions sometimes not being enough. The right course of action for Jackson was to have individual assistance; to have a multidisciplinary team hashing out every detail of planning and programming; and yes, to employ restraint, but only as necessary for safety.

It is a premature rush to judgment to say no one ever needs to be restrained. "Safety," as my friend, the late Jose Martinez-Diaz said, "has to always be the first consideration." For those who harm themselves, the potential of losing functionality and permanently damaging body parts, or compromising or perhaps losing their own lives because of the severity of their behaviors, necessitates immediate and careful considerations.

We were not rash. We had several checks and balances, but restraining another person is a difficult thing to do, a disturbing thing to see happen, and something I never quite got used to as a behavior analyst. Yet when I hear well-intentioned people call for eliminating the use of restraints, I am left wondering what the alternatives are for people like Jackson. Would it really be better to have to repeatedly sedate him with heavy doses of tranquilizers?

My caution in advocating against the abolition of restraint comes from my time with Jackson. Toward the end of my time in residential treatment, the agency accrediting the center disallowed the use of restraint—including the use of an unlocked timeout room, which was an effective treatment that did not involve restraint for some clients with severe aberrant behavior. The change was immediate, and the edict came without any guidance or provision about what to do instead.

When discussing more stringent procedures, people have a tendency to say, "Use it as a last resort," which is ambiguous and unhelpful. I still do not know what that means or how to say I have done "everything else." Everything? Who does everything? I did what I could. I did what I knew to do. I consulted other, more experienced clinical team members. But "everything" probably eluded me.

If attempting to reduce severe problem behavior and assisting in developing adaptive repertoires is not already challenging enough, the "how to" guide is fluid. Adaption to ever-changing rules, evolving best practices, and cultural movements makes working with the silent and individuals with severe aberrant behavior not for the faint of heart. The best we can do is be adaptive, put our best foot forward, discern whether we are doing the right thing, study the salient scientific literature, consult others, and attempt at least a few interventions (while collecting data) before we conclude the approaches we utilized are not working. If the person is suffering and at risk for harm, we must do what we can to keep that person safe. The most fundamental question to ask in serving the silent is "How do I keep this person safe?"

This early part of my career was an incredibly challenging time. I wish I had the knowledge, experience, and ethics I have now. While far from the first person I worked with, Jackson was my first client as a behavior analyst. He was certainly one of my great teachers. I know I gave him a lot of effort. There is a piece of me that feels a little guilty, even though I think I gave what I had and did what I thought was right. I hope he knows I tried as hard as I could with what I knew.

There was no single moment of clarity, but over time, I had the stark realization that Jackson was always going to be living in some type of supported facility. In spite of having an entire team of committed professionals, his learning—and he did learn—took longer than many and his behaviors required him to be living in an environment that could support both safety and nurturance.

When I left residential treatment to begin working as a behavior analyst for my local school district, Jackson was still at the residential treatment center. It was there that he remained for several years until he aged out and moved to a facility for adults. I often wonder what happened to Jackson. Did he learn to cope better with the world? Was the world being kind to him? Was his self-injury reduced to the point that he was no longer a threat to himself? Did the aggressive behavior diminish and his communication extend beyond the seven or eight ASL terms he learned during my time with him?

I think of Jackson often and hope that he is doing well. I hope wherever he is, people are kind and patient with him. I hope that his family still makes time to remind him how important he is to them. I hope other professionals find him as intriguing, funny, and wonderful as I did.

CHAPTER 15

Mr. A. Number 1

Failing to adopt a scientific vantage point and eschewing behavioral science can produce deleterious consequences for the silent. ABA is not a therapy. It is applying the scientific method to problems of particular relevance for a person. The application of this science has a body of evidence that has no equal among helping professions for the silent. Our clients are not "subjects," though. They are children, siblings, friends, and neighbors. Approaching them with anything but unconditional positive regard can compromise the relationship.

Mr. A. Number 1 was one of my favorite kids because he regarded me less as his therapist and more as his assistant. He called me Mr. A. Number 2 and himself Mr. A. Number 1 because we both had first names starting with A. It was not an attempt at humor, but it was downright humorous. I do not use the term "kid" often because the people detailed in this book are no longer children. At the time, though, Mr. A. Number 1 *was* a kid: a kid who would be let down by a state, an educational system, and a support network who steered away from ABA to move to cognitive- and pharmacological-oriented treatments.

As you read his story, know that we had copious amounts of data showing an almost complete elimination of problem behaviors and a huge increase in communicative and academic-related skills. Everything said, "Continue with ABA." Mr. A. Number 1, though, encountered resistance by people who thought they knew better. And, sadly, he paid the price. His story is difficult to tell because he made tremendous, measurable, verifiable progress only to have that progress ruined by systems that did not promote science-based, evidence-based practices.

• • •

"Mr. A. Number 2, are we there yet?"

The plane had just taken off from the airport. Ahead of us were several hours of flight time. After turning his head and facing forward, the self-named Mr. A. Number 1 turned back to me and said, "Are we almost there?"

The journey had just begun.

My long-standing optimism persists even though life can be decidedly cruel. Mr. A. Number 1 had been born with a rare genetic disorder; raised in a loving but tumultuous home; and lived in an area with few experts in evaluating, treating, and educating children with severe problem behavior. The genetic condition included an intellectual impairment; a stumbling block to learning was a common factor affecting almost all of the silent who have graced my life.

How this affliction manifested in Mr. A. Number 1 was a bit unusual. He was consumed with fantasy, and much of how he interacted with the world involved him talking like comic books or shows; talking like make-believe characters, talking about characters; and walking and moving as if he were part of the movies, shows, cartoons, and comics he loved. He was most interested in and often talked as if he were a superhero, more specifically, one of the Mighty Morphin Power Rangers®.

Walking through the unit, the classroom halls, or outside, he would assume what he believed was a martial-arts stance, with his legs spread wide apart and his hands up in chopping positions. "I am a Power Ranger®!" he would say as he sliced and kicked through the air.

He would often assume this persona when he was asked to do classwork or chores. First, he would steadfastly refuse, "I am not going to pick up my clothes, and you can't make me!" This would be followed by a loud "Nooooooo!!!" When staff would approach him, he would summon his alter ego and kick and hit toward them, rarely making contact or harming anyone, as his attempts at violence were a far cry from actually being violent.

Mr. A. Number 1 loved cartoons and comics. When he came to the center, it was apparent he could not easily see the television nor the figures in the books, as his gaze was rarely oriented in the right direction. A collateral effect of his condition was a progression toward blindness. At the young age of 12, his vision was fading, the shows and images he enjoyed and the faces of the people he liked and loved quickly becoming only memories.

Mr. A. Number 1 lived at the center far from his home, a home where he longed to be. In this regard, some of his impairment affecting his knowledge and awareness of certain things may have been a blessing, as his home life had been frenzied. One would never know that when talking with him. He would weave through stories about delicacies sold close to his home and the love he had for his mother and brother, and he made constant queries about when he would return home. It sounded idyllic. He'd say, "Mr. A. Number 2, if I behave, I am going back home to see my mother

Jane in Whack-a-Moe and will get some spamishooobee." None of us knew what most of this meant, though we would eventually learn. It was clear that he had certainly been loved, yet the personal struggles of a single parent wrestling with addiction, the lack of qualified and competent staff within the school system, and a state with few experts in ABA had created a chaotic home life and school experience. Unable to handle his problem behaviors, with property destruction being the most intensive of his behaviors, his mother had little choice but to send him far from the small town where he lived. Thus, he came to the center.

Mr. A. Number 1 lived with other children on the autism unit and then, when he progressed, in our group home. Mr. A. Number 1 was hardly silent. He was loud. He screamed almost as much as he talked. And he talked *a lot*. He had no filter, and when he was denied whatever thing he wanted right away, he would demand and scream, scream and demand. With the expertise available at the unit, we were quickly able to evaluate and put together interventions to address these behaviors successfully. This is not to say we cured him or that the behaviors never happened.

One weekend, I was walking in the local mall. As I approached a music store, I could see several children sitting on the ground and could hear lots of vocal exchanges. As I got closer, I realized the children were from the center. Standing in the middle of the sitting children, screaming at the top of his lungs, was Mr. A. Number 1: "I am tired of sitting here! I want lunch and I am not going to just sit!"

A single staff member was attempting to redirect him while monitoring the other children. A few moments prior, one of the clients, George, had attempted to steal a CD, and when a physically tiny staff member confronted the much larger and violent teenager, he punched her in the face. Her eye was purple and swollen shut by the time I arrived. The store manager and a shopper had jumped up and restrained him, while another person called the police. The remaining staff had to corral the other children, help the injured staff member, and try to calm the melee.

As I walked in, the staff implored Mr. A. Number 1 to sit down, so he screamed louder: "No one can make me sit down! I am hungry! I am tired of being here!"

I said, "Mr. A. Number 1, what do you think you're doing?"

He plopped down on the ground and said, "Oh my God, I'm so sorry. I've missed you, Mr. A. Number 2, so I'll just sit down now and wait here."

There was a crisis to get through, but for the moment, it could be addressed more quietly.

Mr. A. Number 1's behaviors could rankle the teachers and staff at the center, but for whatever reason, not the least of which was the elevated status and nickname he assigned me, we got along. Whereas other people may have thought he was obnoxious, I thought he was charming. His rapid, constant talking was an abrupt change from the majority of clients at the center. I like to think I did not have favorites, but we are all human, and certain clients touch you more deeply than others.

Mr. A. Number 1 seemed to enjoy time with the staff more than time spent with his peers. He was particularly fond of the children on our unit who did not speak—the silent. This may have given him more opportunities to be the only one speaking, a role he coveted, but it endeared me to him even more.

And again, because of the nickname, I think I was one of Mr. A. Number 1's favorites. We had our battles, though. They usually revolved around a simple hygiene task or a basic house chore. While Mr. A. Number 1 didn't yell at me often, he would say, "I'm just not going to do it!" and place his pointer fingers in his ears, making noise to avoid listening. He would then try to wait me out. It was a battle of wills I couldn't lose. Sticking to my script, I would say, "Mr. A. Number 1, I will just wait until you are ready," and repeat whatever the direction was every 2 minutes. This procedure, still premised on kindness and patience, almost always worked. Mr. A. Number 1 could only wait out about 15 minutes before being ready to concede and move on.

Moving on, though, did not come without its own issues. While doing the task he had protested, he would berate the person who dared ask him to do something simple. "This is soooo stupid," he would grumble. With my special status, Mr. A. Number 1 reserved his most dramatic rants for me: "Mr. A. Number 2, I am mad at you! This is ridiculous! You are fired! And you are not going to fly with me back home! I will not let you meet my mother! You will not be my therapist!" Whatever his feelings in the moment, they were fleeting. I had to remain by and near him, as his therapist, to ensure he was safe.

He had said the two things he thought would cut me to the bone: no contact with him nor seeing his mom. After about 30 minutes, he would decide he wanted me to remain his therapist and we could continue to work together: "Oh, Mr. A. Number 2, I'm so sorry. I didn't mean it, OK?"

"It's OK, Mr. A. Number 1. We are good," I would assure him.

It was easy to move on despite the realization it would likely happen again. My empathy and patience for him never wavered. As he progressively lost the ability to see the images, I would read and describe the comics to him. Our psychiatrist explained that the progression of his condition limited his visual acuity and peripheral vision. What he could see was tunneled, blurry, and turning ever darker. For whatever reason, we did not prepare him for blindness. When I look back on it, I don't think we thought it through the way we should have. We were so hyper-focused on his behavior, when the behaviors we should have been focusing on were those that would begin to address the new limited way he would be experiencing the world.

The state from which he came and would one day return considered him in need of very intensive staffing due to his aggressive behaviors. However, even with his worsening vision issues and clumsiness, he never hurt anyone. He may have been incapable of ever hurting anyone, as a heavyset 12-year-old boy who would tear his own shirt but not someone else's, chopping and kicking in the air while proclaiming his superhero might.

For Halloween, one of the staff got him a superhero costume complete with mask and cape. The suit was about two sizes too small, yet he wedged his large body into the little costume and walked around the school and unit all day engaging in various superhero poses. This was not a person who needed to be in a locked down unit, thousands of miles from home.

Fortunately, Mr. A. Number 1 made great strides. His program was designed around the function of his behaviors: aggressive behavior to property no longer produced removal of the task or removal from the area, nor did it result in giving him some item or activity. Staff increased the attention he received when on task or talking appropriately. We waited him out as often as necessary.

It worked.

Data across the board showed decreases in misbehavior and increases in adaptive and academic areas. His was a true success story as he talked more but yelled less. His progress led to transitioning to the group home and contacting his home state to organize his return. What should have been a cause for celebration turned into a worry, and later, a failure. One of the saddest things I ever did was take this child back home.

Mr. A. Number 1 did not move back to his family home: He was placed in a group home. One of my mentors had established a program where before a move, a staff person from the new group home would come to the center to learn the behavior program. Instead, the state sent Mr. A. Number 1's mother to meet with us. Unfortunately, she would not be involved in running his behavior plan, educating him, and teaching him skills in his new residence. As a result, we realized that the staff at the group home would not be able to provide the effective treatment plan we had developed during our time with him. Because of this concern, the center determined that our group home manager and I would fly with him to implement our gradual fading plan and maximize staff training during the first week of his return.

After landing (and having been asked often, "Are we there yet?"), we were hungry and stopped by a gas station to pick up a snack and drink. When we stepped up to the register to pay, there was the magical delicacy Mr. A. Number 1 had told us about: "spamishooobee," aka Spam musubi, a sushi roll made with Spam. Mr. A. Number 1 asked for a piece, so we indulged him. We drove for a while into some low clouds up a mountain; passed a town sounding eerily reminiscent of "Whack-a-Moe"; and arrived at the group home, which sat in close proximity to a psychiatric hospital, one that had reportedly been a place Mr. A. Number 1 had spent some time.

When we arrived at the group home, a psychologist in shorts, a T-shirt, and flip-flops greeted us. Dr. Smith looked like tropical Santa Claus, with long white hair and a thick white beard. He was nice but quickly indicated this was a reality therapy group home, and they would use their techniques to help Mr. A. Number 1. This meant they were going to speak in the abstract, attempt to motivate him intrinsically, and attend to and comment on his problem behavior. This was the opposite of everything that had worked at the center. What he needed and had found success with was concrete language, tangible reinforcers, and minimal attention for problem behavior.

This approach was not a desirable one for Mr. A. Number 1, contraindicated by our assessment and successful treatment data. Mr. A. Number 1 was not some round peg to be forced into a square hole. He had a developmental disability and intellectual impairment, was dealing with the onset of blindness, and talked in a fantasy-like way about being a Power Ranger. How would they get him to face reality? Challenging Mr. A. Number 1 was not the appropriate way to help him. His reality was really difficult. His circumstances were unique, and he had made incredible progress with an individualized assessment and behavior plan. They were expecting him to conform to their program, rather than providing treatment based on his needs, which was setting everyone up for failure.

I cannot fathom what the next few weeks to months were like for him. He went from a place where he was successfully treated and happy to a place where he was frustrated and began screaming again, punching holes in walls, and tearing his clothing. Mr. A. Number 1 did not have to conform to our plan; the plan fit him. Cookie-cutter mental health approaches were never going to work. The lack of a behavioral approach to address his behavior had already resulted in him living thousands of miles away from his home for almost 2 years. They had silenced Mr. A. Number 1 by sending him out of his state to our center, where no one in his own state had to hear him.

When he was at the center, he was a well-prepared person with evidence-based programs with data confirming his progress. Both he and his data spoke loudly of where he was on his personal journey and the potential that existed despite the numerous stumbling blocks placed before him. Mr. A. Number 1 could speak and articulate, but no one was listening.

A few months later, I left the center for a different position and learned Mr. A. Number 1 was back living at the unit, displaying the misbehavior that had dissipated during his first stay.

The system had failed him—again.

Conclusion

I am forever indebted to many, but particularly the silent, for providing so many consequential and wonderful experiences throughout my life. I have told people "I am the world's richest man," and the richness of my life has little to do with money and everything to do with relationships. Relationships, though, are difficult to capture in a book, let alone a single chapter.

Some of the stories you've just read were whimsical, some were hopeful, and others were sad. Each story, regardless of the conveyed emotions, was based on mutually reinforcing relationships. The more emotional stories may camouflage the reality of how much I enjoyed the time spent with these individuals. I found their company comforting and their struggles and triumphs heroic. They made me look forward to going to work each day; observing something new; bearing witness to small changes; and spending the slow, quiet time that occupies most of the time in each of our lives.

When I began my master's degree, only a handful of states had a certification for professionals to work as certified behavior analysts. In 1998, the Behavior Analyst Certification Board (BACB) was formed and offered an international governing body to provide guidelines, educational standards, and ethics for a profession focused on scientific approaches to behavior change, with the long-term goal of each state licensing professionals because such licensing provides the greatest likelihood of affecting and protecting clients (Johnston et al., 2017). Dozens of states now have licensure for behavior analysts. Insurance mandates now cover ABA for individuals on the autism spectrum. In 2001, I became the 515th Board Certified Behavior Analyst® (BCBA®). One of my supervisees was recently certified in the 70,000s. A credential called the Registered Behavior Technician® (RBT®) was created in 2014 to provide minimum standards of training for people interested in this field of work, with over 187,000 RBTs registered at the time of this writing (BACB, 2024). While no perfect system exists, it is now easier to access services and find competent professionals.

Part of telling these stories was that the environmental circumstances that once surrounded the silent largely no longer exist. Institutions have largely been shuttered. Federal education initiatives have led to early education and identification of people with special needs. Early intervention is often sought when children are infants and toddlers, and children begin to receive behavioral, speech-language, and occupational therapy and educational services at earlier ages. Technology continues to emerge that provides opportunities to assist with communication. Tablet devices have applications and programs that produce voice output. A Picture Exchange Communication System (PECS) has been developed. Professionals have successfully employed sign language to teach nonspeaking individuals a way to communicate. Evaluation and intervention happen earlier, increasing the availability of new and better learning opportunities to help improve the quality of life for people with disabilities.

An important article written in 1982, "Toward a Functional Analysis of Self-Injury," was republished in 1994 to reach a wider audience (Iwata et al., 1982/1994). The article ushered in a revolution where pre-intervention assessment procedures were refined, specifically for the silent. Focused on identifying the environmental factors maintaining problem behavior, it meant interventions had a remarkable chance of succeeding, thereby decreasing the use of punishment-based procedures (Pelios et al., 1999). This was so effective that the process of functional behavior assessment was adopted into the Individuals with Disability Education Act (IDEA), the overarching federal law concerning exceptional student education (Zirkel, 2011).

Things are better for the silent, I am happy to say. The days of being locked away and subjected to involuntary tooth extractions, denied educations, and forced to endure any number of systemic neglect and abuses are becoming part of the past. There is still much work to be done, though. Fad treatments, false causes, and fake cures are constantly pedaled to those desperately seeking to address the lack of progress and to reduce the suffering of their loved ones. Fortunately, there exist organizations such as the Association for Science in Autism Treatment (ASAT; n.d.) and books such as *Autism's False Prophets* (Offit, 2010), *Vaccines Did Not Cause Rachel's Autism* (Hotez, 2018), and *Controversial Therapies for Autism and Intellectual Disabilities* (Foxx & Mulick, 2016) to provide more accurate information to caregivers and professionals. Reliable and verifiable evidence is as vital in our work as in courts of law. An evidence-based approach protects the silent by ensuring the assessments and interventions employed have a history of effectiveness and have been rigorously scrutinized.

Why tell these tales? Many reading this book will never know someone who lived for years in an institution. The people with whom I worked largely cannot tell their own stories. The lives of the silent matter. Except for the people who have passed away, I do not know what happened to several of these individuals. The ethical requirements of confidentiality trump my deep curiosity and prevent me from seeking information about how my clients' lives unfold, and so I am left to my thoughts and wishes. I think about the silent often. My hope is that they are living lives they find fulfilling and they have people in their lives who understand them; people who listen; and people who, when they find silence, will be still and use the incredible power of observation to deduce what is going on. I hope their environments are rich with their own, preferred reinforcers; that they are making choices; and that the life in front of them is filled with the noise of laughter or the echoes of their smiles ringing beyond the silence.

References

Anthony, N., & Leff, A. M. (1979). The state mental hospital: A local health department's role. *American Journal of Public Health, 69*(1), 64–67. https://doi.org/10.2105/ajph.69.1.64

Association for Science in Autism Treatment. (n.d.). https://asatonline.org/

Behavior Analyst Certification Board. (2024). *BACB certificant data*. Retrieved November 8, 2024, from https://www.bacb.com/BACB-certificant-data/

Castillo, M. I., Clark, D. R., Schaller, E. A., Donaldson, J. M., DeLeon, I. G., & Kahng, S. (2018). Descriptive assessment of problem behavior during transitions of children with intellectual and developmental disabilities. *Journal of Applied Behavior Analysis, 51*(1), 99–117. https://doi.org/10.1002/jaba.430

Civil Rights Act of 1964, Pub. L. No. 88-352, 78 Stat. 241 (1964). https://www.govinfo.gov/content/pkg/STATUTE-78/pdf/STATUTE-78-Pg241.pdf

Foxx, R. M., & Mulick, J. A. (Eds.). (2016). *Controversial therapies for autism and intellectual disabilities: Fad, fashion, and science in professional practice*. Routledge.

Green, G. (1994). Facilitated communication: Mental miracle or sleight of hand? *Behavior and Social Issues, 4*(1–2), 69–85. https://doi.org/10.5210/bsi.v4i1.209

Hotez, P. J. (2018). *Vaccines did not cause Rachel's autism: My journey as a vaccine scientist, pediatrician, and autism dad*. Johns Hopkins University Press.

Iwata, B. A., Dorsey, M. F., Slifer, K. J., Bauman, K. E., & Richman, G. S. (1994). Toward a functional analysis of self-injury. *Journal of Applied Behavior Analysis, 27*(2), 197–209. https://doi.org/10.1901/jaba.1994.27-197 (Reprinted from "Toward a functional analysis of self-injury," 1982, *Analysis & Intervention in Developmental Disabilities, 2*[1], 3–20, https://doi.org/10.1016/0270-4684(82)90003-9)

Jessel, J., Hanley, G. P., & Ghaemmaghami, M. (2016). A translational evaluation of transitions. *Journal of Applied Behavior Analysis, 49*(2), 359–376. https://doi.org/10.1002/jaba.283

Johnston, J. M., Carr, J. E., & Mellichamp, F. H. (2017). A history of the professional credentialing of applied behavior analysts. *The Behavior Analyst, 40*(2), 523–538. https://doi.org/10.1007/s40614-017-0106-9

Krantz, P. J., & McClannahan, L. E. (1993). Teaching children with autism to initiate to peers: Effects of a script-fading procedure. *Journal of Applied Behavior Analysis, 26*(1), 121–132. https://doi.org/10.1901/jaba.1993.26-121

Luczynski, K. C., & Rodriguez, N. M. (2015). Assessment and treatment of problem behavior associated with transitions. In F. D. D. Reed & D. D. Reed (Eds.), *Autism service delivery: Bridging the gap between science and practice* (pp. 151–173). Springer Science + Business Media. https://doi.org/10.1007/978-1-4939-2656-5_5

Montee, B. B., Miltenberger, R. G., & Wittrock, D. (1995). An experimental analysis of facilitated communication. *Journal of Applied Behavior Analysis, 28*(2), 189–200. https://doi.org/10.1901/jaba.1995.28-189

Offit, P. A. (2010). *Autism's false prophets: Bad science, risky medicine, and the search for a cure.* Columbia University Press.

Pelios, L., Morren, J., Tesch, D., & Axelrod, S. (1999). The impact of functional analysis methodology on treatment choice for self-injurious and aggressive behavior. *Journal of Applied Behavior Analysis, 32*(2), 185–195. https://doi.org/10.1901/jaba.1999.32-185

U.S. Department of Education. (n.d.). *Individuals with Disabilities Education Act: Topic areas.* https://sites.ed.gov/idea/topic-areas/

U.S. Office of Special Education Programs. (2007, July 19). *History: Twenty-five years of progress in educating children with disabilities through IDEA.* Archived. https://files.eric.ed.gov/fulltext/ED556111.pdf

Wheeler, D. L., Jacobson, J. W., Paglieri, R. A., & Schwartz, A. A. (1993). An experimental assessment of facilitated communication. *Mental Retardation, 31*(1), 49–59.

Zirkel, P. A. (2011). State special education laws for functional behavioral assessment and behavior intervention plans. *Behavioral Disorders, 36*(4), 262–278. https://doi.org/10.1177/019874291103600405

ABOUT THE AUTHOR
Andrew Houvouras, MA, BCBA

The phrase "Science is a gift to humanity" encapsulates the appreciation Andrew Houvouras has for science in general, and in particular, the many benefits derived from the science of human behavior, applied behavior analysis (ABA). As a master's student, Andrew was introduced to ABA by his graduate school advisor, Joe Wyatt.

"Like so many clinicians and teachers, I was looking for answers about how I could help people. The books I was reading at the time weren't providing me with the inspiration or answers," he says. "When I learned about ABA, I knew I had found my way."

After graduating, Andrew became a Board Certified Behavior Analyst (BCBA) and began applying behavior science to help reduce problem behavior, teach adaptive skills, and develop systemic changes to promote positive behavior change. Andrew worked with both children and adults in residential treatment and spent over 17 years working in the public school system. He is currently serving as the Director of Experiential Training in the world-renowned School of Behavior Analysis at Florida Institute of Technology.

"As someone who loves ABA, getting to work with bright students and brilliant, committed faculty is an absolute dream come true," he says.

Andrew has long enjoyed writing and is a coauthor of the book *QUICK Responses for Reducing Misbehavior and Suspensions: A Behavioral Toolbox for Classroom and School Leaders*. He consults and speaks nationally and internationally, and he continues to pursue research with his colleagues at Florida Institute of Technology.

An avid surfer, paddleboarder, and bodysurfer, Andrew enjoys hiking, being in or on the water, as well as playing and watching several sports. Baseball has become a favorite pastime, as his sons, Preston and Kooper, both play collegiately. He enjoys reading, movies, and walking the beach to see and photograph sunrises with his French bulldog, Poppy.

Explore more books to support your clinical practice:

The Consulting Supervisor and New Supervisor Workbooks

By Linda A. LeBlanc and Tyra P. Sellers

In this pair of workbooks, Linda LeBlanc and Tyra Sellers continue their efforts to provide useful resources to guide supervision and mentoring.

Discover more from author Andrew Houvouras:

QUICK Responses for Reducing Misbehavior and Suspensions

By Paul Gavoni, Anika Costa, Eric Gormley, Andrew Houvouras, and Frank Krukauskas

Empower your school to tackle misbehavior systematically. Discover actionable tools to enhance student behavior and achievement through unified, practical approaches to classroom and school-wide management.

www.KeyPressPublishing.com

www.ingramcontent.com/pod-product-compliance
Lightning Source LLC
Chambersburg PA
CBHW070626030426
42337CB00020B/3931